EFFECTIVE
HIRING

HarperCollins
LEADERSHIP

An Imprint of HarperCollins

EFFECTIVE
HIRING

MASTERING THE INTERVIEW,
OFFER, AND ONBOARDING

PAUL FALCONE

Published by HarperCollins Leadership, an imprint of HarperCollins Focus LLC.

Published in association with Kevin Anderson & Associates: https://www.ka-writing.com/.

Topic 8: From "The Emotionally Intelligent Interviewer: A Smarter Questioning Strategy." *SHRM HR Daily Newsletter*, March 23, 2021. Copyright 2021 by the Society for Human Resource Management. **Topic 9:** From "Interviewing a Technical Candidate When You're Not a Techie." *SHRM HR Daily Newsletter*, July 7, 2020. Copyright 2020 by the Society for Human Resource Management. **Topic 10:** From "Interviewing Remote Employees: How to Measure and Manage the Unseen." *SHRM HR Daily Newsletter*, July 19, 2018. Copyright 2018 by the Society for Human Resource Management. **Topic 11:** From "Interviewing and Evaluating Freelancers: The New Frontier of Hiring Just-in-Time and Virtual Talent." *SHRM HR Daily Newsletter*, July 18, 2018. Copyright 2018 by the Society for Human Resource Management. **Topic 14:** From "Interviewing the Boss: 12 Intelligent Questions to Ask to Politely Assess Your Next Manager." *SHRM HR Daily Newsletter*, August 1, 2018. Copyright 2018 by the Society for Human Resource Management. All of the above used by permission of the publisher. All rights reserved.

ISBN 978-1-4002-3009-9 (eBook)
ISBN 978-1-4002-3003-7 (TP)

Library of Congress Control Number: 2021951208

Printed in the United States of America
22 23 24 25 26 LSC 10 9 8 7 6 5 4 3 2 1

CONTENTS

INTRODUCTION

One of the most important responsibilities and opportunities that comes along with leadership lies in hiring the right people for the jobs in your company. Whether you're an executive vice president or a first-time supervisor, your individual performance directly reflects your team's productivity. If you hire the right people who are self-motivated, have a high level of self-awareness, and hold themselves accountable for bottom-line results, your career should sail happily along while building and growing the careers of those following in your footsteps. Conversely, if you hire the wrong people, you'll spend considerable time counseling and disciplining workers who struggle just to meet minimum expectations. Often, you will be forced to do the work yourself—at the expense of your family time, your social life, and your sleep.

Self-motivated new hires find new ways of handling the workflow, assume broader responsibilities beyond their basic job description, and do their best work every day—with little need for your intervention. You recognize these workers when you see them: they typically stand out from their peers in terms of their willingness to assume additional responsibilities; take creative approaches to their work based on their natural, healthy sense of curiosity; appreciate the opportunity you've given them; and behave with gratitude. If you can find these kinds of hires for every job opening, you'll be well ahead of your peers and develop a reputation as a team builder and people developer.

Unfortunately, many leaders in corporate America become jaded over the course of their careers. They reason that finding exceptional hires is more a matter of chance than planned strategy, and they're so busy doing their day-to-day work that they often don't pay enough attention to the open positions they're responsible for filling. Then again, that becomes a self-fulfilling prophecy of downward spiraling because if you don't take the time to fill the open positions on your team, then you and the rest of your group become overburdened making up for the talent shortage and often plunge into a tailspin that will soon lead to burnout.

My goal is to change your perspective on the hiring and selection process. To achieve this, you'll need to make a leap of faith with me on two critical fronts: First, with the tools in this book that you're about to access, you must believe that you can catapult your candidate-evaluation skills to new heights and become a magnet for top-notch talent. Second, no matter what exigencies lie before you at any given time, you have to commit to filling openings on your team as your top-most priority under all circumstances. To do anything less isn't fair to you or the other members of your team.

In short, you're only as good as the people you hire. Let's venture together now and determine what new approaches and tools for recruitment and hiring are available to you as you address this critical leadership responsibility head-on.

DISCLAIMER

Note: Throughout this book, I interchange the use of *his* and *her*, and I provide examples of fictitious men and women. Obviously, all situations described in these pages can apply to anyone. Further, please bear in mind at all times that this book is not intended as a legal guide. Because the book does not purport to render legal advice, it should not be used in place of a licensed practicing attorney when proper legal counsel and guidance become necessary. You must rely on your attorney to render a legal opinion that is related to actual fact situations.

PART 1

PREPARING TO LAUNCH YOUR CANDIDATE SEARCH

This chapter covers what you need to know *before* you even begin recruiting or interviewing potential new hires. First, decide what's most important to you regarding the people you bring into your organization: What do you value most? Determine this before you even begin recruiting. Then, I offer some guidelines to how you can enhance your recruiting process by leveraging four different resources: contingency search firms, headhunters, firms to which you can outsource the entire recruiting process, and outplacement firms (which are helping downsized employees find new jobs). I'll also describe how you can recruit directly, using your own network. Finally, the chapter provides some preliminary questions you might ask job candidates as well as tips on how to screen potential interviewees over the phone before spending a longer time bringing in candidates for a full, in-person interview.

CRITERIA TO HELP YOU DEFINE
THE BEST AND BRIGHTEST TALENT

Before you even begin your search for people to join your organization, it's important to define your key criteria for evaluating resumes and selecting finalists to come in to interview. This section describes the four key attributes I look for and why; feel free to choose your own. Before you delve into isolating the core competencies for a particular position and generating behavior-based questions that highlight those competencies, you need to identify *your* values that drive your recruitment and selection efforts. Once you've done that, you then need to determine which interview questions help you determine whether a particular candidate meets those criteria.

LONGEVITY

Longevity represents the potential return on investment from a new hire relative to your involvement in that individual's onboarding and training. In many cases, candidates' resumes display a rhythm or cadence in terms of how long they remain with companies (barring exceptional circumstances that are outside candidates' control, such as layoffs). Therefore, when interviewing candidates, focus on their reasons for leaving prior positions, because these reasons serve as the link in career progression that defines their values and career management strategies. Most important, ask why they are considering leaving their current company and how your organization can fill the need they are trying to achieve.

If the reason is because of layoffs, always distinguish between group layoffs and individual layoffs. Group layoffs can impact hundreds or even thousands of people, so that's clearly a no-harm, no-foul reason for leaving a company. But if employees appear to be individually selected for layoff, that could be a red flag: companies may be opting to lay off specific individuals and offer a severance package as an alternative to pursuing progressive discipline and structuring a termination for cause. Likewise, if a candidate can explain objectively how the layoff selection criteria were applied without sounding bitter or resentful, those objective career introspection skills may demonstrate a high level of emotional intelligence and business maturity. Finally, if someone survived multiple rounds of layoffs and was the last to leave and asked to "shut the lights off" on the last day, that could speak to a high level of trust and loyalty from the organization and weigh very favorably in that person's candidacy.

When candidates orchestrate their own moves and point to the most common response, "No room for growth," challenge their interpretation of what growth means to them. For some, it may mean promotion to higher levels of responsibility, and for others it may mean a lateral assumption of increased responsibilities (for example, an overseas rotation or exposure to other parts of the business). Still others view growth potential strictly in terms of salary increases and believe they're not paid their market worth. Candidates who expect your company (or any employer) to make up for their failure or inability to maintain market pay parity are making a mistake. It's not your organization's job to help restore candidates to their perceived level of market worth. So be wary of candidates expecting salary increases in excess of 20 percent.

PROGRESSION THROUGH THE RANKS

To identify and highlight candidates' penchants for promoting through the ranks, ask:

Walk me through your progression in your career, leading me up to how you landed in your current company and role.

This question cuts right to the chase. It helps candidates frame their entire resume, demonstrating where they began and how they got to their present company and level of responsibility. It also helps you gauge their ability to summarize large blocks of information succinctly and accurately.

What if a candidate began in the role of controller eight years ago and is still in that role (that is, there has been no vertical progression)? Of course, that's absolutely fine in terms of the candidate's credentials—who wouldn't want someone with eight years of dedicated service to a particular role within the same company? But this question itself may imply that there should be some sort of upward progression, and candidates may be embarrassed or feel bad about not being able to answer it within that context.

To allow for an easy out, simply add a follow-up question like this:

It's great that you've been in your role for eight years. Let me ask you this: How has your role changed over the years, and how have you had to reinvent your job in light of your company's changing needs?

That follow-up question goes a long way in allowing the candidate to respond in a different way and explain the many challenges faced over that period of time and how the candidate adapted to them.

TECHNICAL SKILLS AND EDUCATION

Technical skills and education provide a foundation that helps justify hiring one candidate over another. After all, if candidates have the right software or equipment skills, medical licensure, educational certification, and the like, they certainly qualify on paper as finalists for the position. But like all things in life, having the paper certificate or the background experience alone doesn't tell you much about how well they perform in a particular area or how they approach their work on a day-to-day basis. Also, it's perfectly acceptable to state, "Please answer this in layman's terms, as I don't have my degree in microbiology," or something similar. Candidates will always try to accommodate your requests for a simple explanation, as long as you volunteer your shortcomings up front and transparently. Therefore, engage candidates by asking questions such as this:

> On a scale of one to ten, with ten being a perfect match for this position based on your current understanding, how would you rate yourself from a technical standpoint?

Expect a typical response of eight; most candidates won't tell you they're a ten because they don't want to come across as arrogant or as a know-it-all, but they probably won't grade themselves below a seven for fear that you'll screen them out as underqualified.

Your follow-up question, then, would logically be:

> Okay, tell me why you're an eight, and what would make you a ten?

Asking the question this way allows candidates to highlight their skills gap and explain why accepting this position would help them learn new things and be motivated by the role. Additional follow-up questions might then be:

Where do you think you'll need the most structure, direction, and feedback in your first 90 or 180 days?

Why would you consider accepting this position as a good move in progression from a career development standpoint?

Again, ask candidates to explain why they want to join your organization, what motivates them most, and why they see this opportunity as an excellent move overall within the context of their own career management planning. It's a healthy opening exercise for any interview, and candidates generally appreciate your transparent interviewing style because you're helping them connect the dots in their own career development.

PERSONALITY MATCH/X-FACTOR/PERSONAL CHEMISTRY

This criterion is often misleading. We all tend to hire in our own image, but initial likability doesn't necessarily equate with compatibility on the job. Since many managers tend to hire people they initially like and hit it off with, be careful not to make this your first criterion; make it your last. Compatibility is such a key element of successful new hires that it can't be understated how important this "matching" feature is. Simply put, a successful headhunter or in-house recruiter knows how to match an individual's personality and workstyle to the culture of the organization, department, or unit where that candidate will be working. When the fit works naturally and seamlessly, the chances of a new hire's success skyrocket. It's totally within your control to develop a "fit factor" mindset and approach to candidate selection from this point forward in your career. Even more important—it's fun and exciting.

Only use this issue as a swing factor once you've delved into the first three objective criteria in a diagnostic and dispassionate manner. I address "personality" and "personal style" further in chapter 4 because it's important to understand that the glue that binds someone to a particular job or company is emotional in nature more than it is technical or cognitive. Therefore, this aspect of your interview-questioning strategy will play a critical role toward the end of the interviewing process. You'll also have a chance to confirm your initial instincts with a candidate's prior supervisors during the reference checking process and before you extend an offer of employment.

2

MAXIMIZING YOUR RECRUITMENT RESOURCES

Selecting outside organizations to help you identify and approach high-performance job candidates can be highly effective if you know how best to use their services. Following is a brief description of four types of resources you might consider.

OPTION ONE:
CONTINGENCY SEARCH FIRMS

There are two types of contingency recruiters: administrative support recruiters and professional/technical search recruiters. Traditional administrative support agencies place administrative assistants, staff accountants, customer services representatives, and the like: job candidates generally earn $75,000 a year and under. In contrast, professional/technical agencies usually specialize in individual disciplines, such as accounting and finance, data analytics and IT, retail, software engineering, and pharmaceutical sales, in which candidates typically earn between $65,000 and $125,000 a year.

Both types operate on contingency, meaning they get paid only if you, the client, hire one of their candidates. Contingency recruiters earn a fee based on a percentage of a candidate's annual salary, typically 1 percent per thousand dollars of the candidate's first-year earnings, to a maximum of 33 percent. For example, if you're a semiconductor manufacturer looking for an early-career sales engineer who earns $85,000 a year, then your fee to a contingency recruiter who successfully finds someone for you is $28,050, or 33 percent of $85,000.

Contingency search firms also offer a safety-net guarantee period in case a candidate doesn't work out in the first quarter. Those guarantees usually come in the form of a thirty-day free trial period (where the fee you paid is totally refunded) and a ninety-day candidate-replacement period (where the agency replaces the candidate at no additional cost). Fees and guarantee periods may be negotiable, depending on your market and the demand for the particular types of candidates you're pursuing.

The search firms that are the most successful at meeting clients' demands flourish. Therefore, working with contingency recruiters is a win-win situation: you pay only if you hire their candidate and the individual remains with your organization for a minimum period of time (i.e., through the initial trial period).

OPTION TWO:
RETAINED-SEARCH FIRMS, OR HEADHUNTERS

The retained-search business is much more exclusive than contingency search firms. Retained recruiters typically target candidates earning $100,000 and up. For example, if a semiconductor manufacturer is looking for a general manager with an MBA and ten or more years of power electronics experience in the international arena to become part of a $20 million company with eight hundred employees, then a retained recruiter would bid for the business and begin the search.

Of course, there might only be fifty or a hundred people in the whole country who meet your exacting criteria. That means that the headhunter would have to spend a great deal of time researching your competition, developing names and profiles of candidates, approaching those individuals with your opportunity, and then qualifying them in terms of their willingness and ability to do the job, to fit your company's corporate culture, and to potentially relocate.

These recruiters work on retainer and traditionally get paid in three installments: one-third of the fee initially to begin the search, one-third after thirty days, and one-third after sixty days—regardless of whether the search is completed. You are paying for their time and expertise in researching, sourcing, and proactively qualifying candidates who are not necessarily currently on the job market. In-house human resources recruiters typically lack the time and resources you may need in urgent situations for executive-level talent; also, they may not have the experience or technical expertise to land such senior-level candidates. As such, outsourcing to a third-party consultant may make sense in such hard-to-fill scenarios.

The bottom line: employ a retained search firm for six-figure positions with exacting criteria when your sense of urgency is great and your need for dedicated attention is critical. If you find it difficult to pay a retainer when contingency recruiters will apparently do the same work for free, remember that it wouldn't make as much sense for contingency recruiters to work a search assignment that's too difficult when they have other, more fillable openings to tend to. Retained recruiters, in comparison, will be beholden to you until the assignment is completed because they will already have been paid their fee.

OPTION THREE:
RECRUITMENT PROCESS OUTSOURCE (RPO) PROVIDERS

With this approach, an organization outsources its recruitment function to a third party. This makes most sense in cases where high-volume openings make it more cost efficient to source, interview, and onboard candidates with the help of an external provider (think procurement warehouses where hundreds of new hires may be required at any given time).

Actually, any company that hires ten or more workers per month could benefit from the services of an RPO provider. RPO firms attempt to offer more efficient recruitment services for their client companies, and their ultimate goal is to lower your company's cost per hire and allow your organization to focus on its core strengths and business competencies.

Recruitment outsourcing services can also make sense if you work in an industry that has fluctuating hiring demands or in cases where you want to be prepared for a volatile labor market. For example, when a business downturn hits and recruiting needs suddenly drop, so does a company's need for recruiting staff. Likewise, when a business finds itself suddenly expanding, recruiting needs may suddenly spike. Outsourcing the recruitment function allows your company to pass along the risk to the RPO provider, which offers flexibility, economies of scale, and greater access to potential talent pools.

RPO providers differ greatly from contingent and retained-search providers because an RPO provider functions as your internal recruitment department: it manages your entire recruiting process and is responsible for the results. Your contract can spell out specific recruitment-related functions that you want to outsource, or you can outsource the entire recruitment function as a package offering.

RPO firms can use their own employees or your company's staff, technology, methodologies, and reporting. Therefore, it's difficult to approximate their costs, which depend on how much of the process you intend to outsource and whether you choose to retain recruiters on your payroll or outsource them. (There are a variety of fee models that are beyond the scope of this book.)

Whether an RPO solution makes sense for your organization will depend on whether you're comfortable working under an exclusive agreement for outsourcing recruiting for your entire organization, a specific hiring drive, or a known project length. It will require an in-depth, holistic look at your current cost per hire, retention and turnover statistics, and overall caliber of talent hired.

RPOs tend to work exceptionally well with small to mid-sized client organizations, especially those growing quickly. Some of the biggest recruiting challenges organizations face include finding talent, hiring manager satisfaction, managing the candidate experience, responding to scalability needs, performance reporting, and developing and maintaining the employment brand. As a broader trend gaining momentum in corporate America, the RPO option could certainly be worth a closer look.

OPTION FOUR:
OUTPLACEMENT FIRMS' JOB DEVELOPMENT DEPARTMENTS

Outplacement firms are paid by companies that are downsizing (because of mergers, acquisitions, or bankruptcies) to assist displaced workers in finding jobs.

It's in the outplacement firm's best interests to place its candidates as quickly as possible, because it costs the firms lots of money to provide services for displaced executives, including office and telephone access, word-processing support for cover letters and resumes, and administrative and training support. It's estimated that if a senior-level candidate remains on the outplacement firm's books for more than six months, the outplacement firm loses money on that transaction.

When companies downsize because of mergers, acquisitions, or bankruptcies, for example, certain affected workers may be offered some form of outplacement services in exchange for signing a full release of claims (typically including severance packages and benefits continuation for a limited time). Fees are often tiered depending on the level of the employee involved and the length of the outplacement program.

This service is relevant to you during recruitment because the outplacement firm is paid by the candidate's former company, not by you (the potential new employer), so this free supply of talent could significantly reduce your cost per hire. If you're unsure of this source because you feel that the candidates from outplacement firms are the ones who couldn't make the cut, don't be. Companies have downsized entire divisions in this era of mergers, acquisitions, and divestitures, and many of the candidates now in outplacement's care were being placed by retained search not so long ago. If the outplacement provider does not have a job development department, simply ask if they can post your opening on their internal proprietary job board. Outplacement firms can be an incredible source of free, highly qualified talent, and investing in a few relationships with several firms might be a smart business decision.

SPECIAL NOTE

Diversity recruitment outreach sources can help you fine-tune your search as well. Where you recruit is important, and expanding your reach to niche job sites like the following can help strengthen diversity among your selection pool and new hire ranks as well as provide your organization with a higher profile in diverse communities. These sources are a good place to start, but there are many more:

DiversityJobs.com

LatinoJobs.org

OverFiftyJobs.com

DisabilityJobs.net

BlackCareers.org

AsianHires.com

NativeJobs.org

LGBTjobsite.com

VeteranJobs.net

WeHireWomen.com

Further, if you work with a recruitment advertising agency, they can often build in diversity outreach sites to the standard advertising package you order through them. There's so much more to diversity, equity, and inclusion, and it's such a broad topic that this section doesn't begin to address its many facets. Still, raising awareness about where you post your jobs and broadening your community reach with the help of these and other dedicated websites can go a long way in expanding your diversity recruitment efforts.

DIRECT SOURCING

ALTERNATIVES TO TRADITIONAL CANDIDATE OUTREACH

While professional networking tools (such as LinkedIn) allow employers to proactively identify and source "passive" candidates (that is, those not necessarily in job search mode at the time of contact), there are advantages to approaching potential job candidates by phone rather than electronically:

- You may gain access to a potential pool of talented workers who may not be looking for a new job but may be open to hearing about new opportunities;
- You'll reduce your hiring costs if your outreach efforts succeed;
- You'll gain an opportunity to network with individuals at competitor firms; and
- You'll generate a sense of self-sufficiency as you develop the skills necessary to proactively reach out to and develop talent that ultimately helps you build your business team and shift the competitive advantage in your favor.

However, there may also be disadvantages to this strategy:

■ If you're perceived as "stealing" from the competition, the competition may feel justified to steal from your organization;

■ Industry relationships could be compromised if old friends at competitor firms find out that your company is perceived to be "raiding" theirs.

In general, therefore, it's best to leave headhunting to headhunters. Still, on a limited basis, it may make sense for frontline managers to carefully develop their own network of recruiting sources at competitor firms; so, let's discuss how you might pursue this option.

Let's assume you're a manager of finance looking to fill a financial analyst position in your department. You would typically post the job internally, run online ads, scour LinkedIn using a keyword search for qualified individuals in your network, and possibly engage the services of a search firm. Before engaging a placement firm, though, you might try a limited telephone outreach to other organizations in your industry or geographical area.

First, make a list of companies that compete directly with yours. Then discuss with your boss and human resources the possibility of your reaching out to your peers at those organizations to introduce yourself and share more about the opening on your team. Full internal transparency is important at this step: if senior leadership or HR dislikes the idea (for example, because it may be an industry taboo), respect their decision and forego this direct outreach approach.

That being said, assuming your company list is approved, and you get the green light to conduct such an outreach, contact those companies and ask the person answering the phone for the name of the manager of finance, whom you would consider your peer.

The receptionist, acting as a "screener" or "gatekeeper," will ask about the purpose of your call. Simply state that you work as the finance manager for XYZ Company, a competitor organization, and you have a networking question for their finance manager and would like that person's help. That should get your call through. Feel free to leave your name and telephone number if the individual isn't available at the time of your call. (Just be sure to write the person's name down so that when your call is returned, you'll remember who it is!)

Let's look at how these calls play out. When the manager picks up the phone, introduce yourself and your company, then state the purpose of your call. It might sound like this:

Hi, Julia, my name is Paul Falcone, and I'm the manager of finance at XYZ Corporation. I'm doing a friendly outreach to people in my peer group at competitor firms in town to see if they might be able to help us identify a financial analyst candidate for a position we're trying to fill. (At that point, you can share more about the opening, the keys to hire, the softwares required, and the like.) I was wondering if there's anyone in your network who you could recommend, either because they're in career transition right now or otherwise feeling "boxed in" in their current job and might be looking for a new opportunity. I'd be happy to return the favor in the future.

That's a respectful telephone introduction, and it's certainly to the point. The added benefit is that the call will help you build goodwill relations with others in your industry. Remember, by calling your peer, there's nothing intrusive or threatening about the phone call. It really is little more than a goodwill outreach. And don't be surprised if this individual calls you in the future for a similar networking purpose.

There's no mystery to these types of phone calls; they will work only if you're open and honest about your approach to networking with competitors. If five to ten outreach calls to competitor firms in your area generate one or two exploratory interviews, congratulations, you've done well! If your preliminary networking outreach is not successful, then be sure to tell the headhunter you later engage which organizations you've already contacted. That's what smart networking is all about. That being said, always check with your supervisor or department head before you pick up the phone to begin your networking outreach. Some companies prefer not to contact competitors directly under any circumstances, so it's always best to get advance approval from your boss before initiating your outreach.

HIRING IN OUR OWN IMAGE

SOUND TIPS AS WELL AS A CAUTIONARY TALE

Chapter 1 touched on the importance of hiring in our own image. I cautioned, however, that candidates' initial likability doesn't necessarily equate to compatibility on the job, and you should be careful to make the likability factor the last, not the first, criterion in selecting candidates for final interview rounds. It's time to pick up with that topic in more detail because of its critical importance in the candidate selection process.

First, to the "cautionary tale" part of this topic. I've worked both sides of the desk: as a contingency, fee-based recruiter and as a corporate, in-house recruiter. Many times, I saw hiring managers who were ecstatic at a candidate I referred for an interview, after they met with the individual for only ten or fifteen minutes. In every case, I realized the hiring manager didn't really know how to interview or appreciate how to hire. After all, there's so much to an interview that no one can really discern what makes a candidate tick in so little time. Their rush to judgment about how much they liked the applicant was based purely on the likability factor—how much they had in common, how well they got along in their discussions, and how comfortable they immediately felt after the initial introduction.

Ah, but that's the danger of the allure involved in interviewing and hiring. As a hiring manager, you really can't determine how much you like a candidate until you've discerned how compatible you are with one another's communication styles, pace, need for structure, direction, and feedback, ability to accept constructive criticism, and so much more.

In fact, in my search firm days, our research found that about 20 percent of all new hires did not survive their initial trial periods at the companies that hired them (our clients). Why so? We dug deeper, followed up with the client companies' hiring managers and human resource recruitment teams, and learned that new hires fell off before the ninetieth day not because of lack of technical skills but because of a personality mismatch. Perhaps the new hire was overly sensitive, failed to bond with peers, was unwilling to work the standard operating hours that everyone else followed, or otherwise required too much oversight to work independently. From that point forward, we decided to check for those interpersonal and stylistic issues on the front end of the recruitment process—before ever referring the applicant to the hiring organization. We believed that the real value we provided was in matching the individual's personality to the organization's culture—which is where the real "match" is made.

I've followed that strategy for the rest of my career, with excellent results. As an HR practitioner myself, I've also trained frontline managers on interview-questioning techniques to help them build muscle and critical mass in this key area of their responsibilities. Finally, I invited them to join me during reference-checking telephone calls so they could hear from and speak directly with finalist candidates' former supervisors before making the commitment to hire. Not every hiring manager took me up on my offer, but the ones who did immediately saw the value in that process and often wondered how they got along up to that point in their careers without being part of the reference-checking process themselves.

My best advice: don't rush the process. Hone your own inter-viewing skills and the questions that are meaningful to you. Apply them consistently and connect your interview questions to the que-ries you pose to applicants' former supervisors during the reference-checking process. No, there are no guarantees when hiring candidates to join your company. But you are indeed capable of making "high-probability" hires if you engage in all aspects of the hiring process purposefully and intentionally.

The beauty of the questions that follow is that they can be used in two separate arenas:

■ First, they open the door of communication and transparency with the job candidate.
■ Second, they can then be asked of former supervisors during the reference-checking process.

In other words, these stylistic questions lend themselves to initial candidate responses and then vetting by a third party once all rounds of interviews have been completed (but prior to an actual job offer being extended). Here are questions that lend themselves to this dual-usage format:

What kind of structure and supervision would provide you with the most support from day one? Do you prefer a structured environment with clear guidelines and immediate feedback or more of an autono-mous, independent, "hands-off" type of working relationship with your boss?

In hiring a [job title], we look for a solid balance between quality and quantity in candidates' work. Still, most people lean more in one direction than another. Where do you typically fall on the quality-volume spectrum?

Tell me about your ability to accept constructive criticism. Can your feelings be hurt, and should I be cautious about delivering tougher news, or do you pride yourself on having a thicker skin?

As far as your natural and preferred pace of work, do you function better in

a moderate, controllable, and predictable environment;

a faster-paced atmosphere with deadline pressures and time constraints; or

a "hyperspace," chaotic, "management-by-crisis" culture?

How would you describe your day-to-day approach to working with others? I don't like to use the word *attitude* because it's open to so many different interpretations, but how would people describe your overall demeanor in the workplace? Will people know when you're not having a good day and, if so, how can they tell?

How many hours a week do you find it necessary to work in order to get the job done? There's no right or wrong answer here: I'm just looking for what your historical time commitment has been and what you'd like to see it look like going forward.

Has anyone ever critiqued your reliability or dependability? I'm not asking about absenteeism or tardiness so much, but rather I'm looking more to see how you'd grade yourself in terms of your overall reliability to be present and to accomplish your work projects on time and under budget.

What motivates you most at this point in your career?

Is there anything that typically "unwinds" you or bothers you that you'd like me to know about? On a scale of one to ten, with ten being highest or best, how would you grade yourself in terms of your overall abilities and contributions to the companies where you've worked up to now?

Of course, these questions can be adopted for the type of role you're hiring for. You'll ask different types of questions for salespeople versus PhD research scientists. For example, here are some alternative questions that you might want to ask of potential senior leader candidates:

Would you describe your management style as more autocratic and paternalistic or geared toward a more participative and consensus-building approach?

How do you approach taking action without getting prior approval? Is it your natural inclination to report to someone else for sign-off, or do you prefer to operate more with independent responsibility and authority? Can anyone ever accuse you of asking for forgiveness after the fact rather than asking for permission up front?

Looking back at your past performance over the last few years, how effective have you been at orchestrating a corporate ensemble of functional areas? What area or department got most focus, and which one suffered a bit from benign neglect?

How would you describe your ability to cope with the significant pressures associated with senior management?

Have you ever delayed the inevitable in terms of disciplining or dismissing employees?

Would people describe your ability and willingness to confront problem situations head-on as more aggressive or passive overall?

What are you most known for: communication, teambuilding, or expense management?

What still makes you smile at this point in your career and propels you out of bed and to work each morning?

What's important is that you give thought to what your questions and a candidate's prospective responses might be. Remember that most new-hire failures are not a result of a technical mismatch; early turnover typically results from a difference in core values about leadership, communication, and expectations regarding teamwork. In short, it's the lack of compatible business styles that dooms new hires. Find a way to inject those issues into your early discussions during the interview process, and then confirm your impressions during references. The chances of making a high-probability hire can skyrocket when you take such an honest and transparent approach to candidate evaluation and selection.

5

TELEPHONE SCREENING INTERVIEWS

HOW TO IDENTIFY IF A CANDIDATE
IS WORTH BRINGING INTO THE OFFICE

Telephone screening interviews can be a practical defense to the sheer number of people applying for jobs. Telephone introductions attempt to determine candidate suitability in shorter time frames (ten to fifteen minutes) with less commitment on your part. Many hiring managers say telephone screening cuts down on their in-person interviews by up to 40 percent.

The ease of the telephone evaluation is usually determined by the scope and depth of a person's resume or online profile. The more details, the easier the selection. Still, not all candidates are masters at resume writing or highlighting their achievements on LinkedIn, and you don't want to screen out potential high performers because they're not great at selling themselves on paper. Many hourly or early career candidates only briefly describe their primary job responsibilities without relating them to the achievements and accomplishments they gained for the company while working there. Furthermore, many people don't describe their companies' market niches or size as well as their own straight and dotted-line reporting relationships on paper. That information would obviously make the matching process a lot easier for you, so you'll have to cull it yourself.

There are five major segments of the candidate telephone screen; all five are critical because any one area could knock a candidate out of contention. During the telephone screen, make sure the big items are checked off: if salary expectations are out of whack, if travel restrictions are too limiting, or if the individual won't be available to start with your company for six months because of contractual or personal obligations, now's the time to find out. The information you get in advance will also help prepare for an in-person interview.

KEYS TO HIRE

Identify the top two to three (or three to five) core requirements of the position you're seeking to fill, before making any calls to candidates, to ensure that you and the candidates are on the same page. Much will depend on whether the position is hourly or professional, of course, so at a minimum, check for availability to interview, availability to begin work, commitment to a set schedule (especially if you're hiring for a swing or night shift), software familiarity, and the like. Any major knockout in any one of these areas may disqualify the individual from further consideration.

CANDIDATE'S CORE QUALIFICATIONS

This is your opportunity to match the keys to hire to the individual's core qualifications. Make specific note of any mismatches that may be critical in the selection process—for example, an inability to speak fluent Spanish, the lack of a bachelor's degree, a lack of knowledge of Photoshop or Adobe Creative Suite, and the like. In general, if a candidate doesn't meet two of the top three (or three of the top five) keys to hire, it may be better to continue looking rather than schedule an in-person interview.

Also, depending on the type of role involved, ask candidates about information not typically listed on their resumes or LinkedIn profiles regarding their current company demographics and role specifics, since these are important factors:

■ Publicly traded versus privately held company
■ Company size, either in terms of revenue or the number of employees (or both)
■ Reporting relationship (supervisor's title, direct versus extended reports, size of department): be sure to distinguish between straight and dotted-line reporting relationships, and clarify the numbers and titles of subordinates.

MOTIVATION FOR CHANGE

Ensure that the opportunity your organization offers makes sense for the candidate in the near to intermediate term. Without a healthy match between the candidate's career needs and your company's desire for high performance, consistency, and sustainability, the new relationship may fail.

Keep an eye out for any red-flag responses at this initial stage that may concern you (for example, "My company is considering promoting me, but I'm not sure I want to stay"). Make special note of any hesitations the candidate may have about timing, location, or other pending job offers that may be in play.

COMPENSATION EXPECTATIONS

Whether you can discuss salary history up front or must wait until a conditional employment offer is extended will likely depend on the rules and recent legislation of your state, city, or municipality. Even if you can't discuss salary *history* before making a conditional employment offer because laws in certain states ban it, you may be able to discuss salary *expectations*.

Some employers outline the base salary and other compensation factors (for example, expected overtime, bonus target) up front during this first phone call so that neither party is wasting time by interviewing. Compensation budgets are often preset with little flexibility to go above the stipulated maximum, so it may make sense to get this critical issue off the table right from the start. Be sure to confirm in advance how your organization prefers to handle salary discussions specifically during the telephone screening stage and in general. The new laws that aim to end the cycle of pay discrimination by eliminating inquiries regarding a candidate's pay history have teeth that can bite hard in terms of penalties and damages, so this is something you must get right before you pick up the phone to make your first call.

AVAILABILITY TO BEGIN WORK

This criterion is fairly self-explanatory and obvious, but it's always a good idea during a telephone screen to make sure that the candidate has the appropriate amount of flexibility to match your expectations regarding schedules, shifts, and travel requirements. For more junior-level workers, you'll also want to discuss if the location of your office, warehouse, or laboratory is within a reasonable traveling distance.

Be especially careful here: nonexempt workers who are eager to find a job and earn their next paycheck may be quick to say yes to a job that's fifty miles from home or that will take ninety minutes and three buses to reach one way. Despite their eagerness to join your ranks, longer commutes may not make sense for them over the longer term, and once a similar-paying position becomes available closer to home, they may resign for it. What's a reasonable commute, time to spend in the car, or percentage of air travel will clearly depend on the nature of the role and the potential compensation. It's always worthwhile asking, however, since this can be a deal breaker in the first six months to a year.

INTERVIEWING STRATEGIES AND QUESTIONS TO IDENTIFY "HIGH-PROBABILITY" HIRES

This chapter provides what you need to know to interview *successfully*—since interviewing isn't a skill that's really taught to many executives, managers, and supervisors. The first few sections of this chapter provide general interview guidelines. Then I discuss strategies for interviewing specific types of candidates—technical personnel; remote staff; freelancers and independent contractors; salespeople and business-development people; higher-level supervisors, managers, and directors; and finally, how to interview people who will become your next boss—an art in itself!

THE ANATOMY OF AN EFFECTIVE INTERVIEW

Many people—even high-level executives—have never been educated in how to interview people effectively; many HR managers find that hiring managers often start an interview with a job candidate with statements and questions like these:

Tell me about yourself.

What's your greatest strength?

Give me an example of a time when you've had to overcome a significant obstacle at work.

Often there's little consistency in the questioning techniques of managers in the same company, there are no icebreakers to ease into the interview, and the strategy for what the hiring managers are looking for gets lost in the shuffle.

Going from zero to question-and-answer mode in any interview misses the opportunity to build rapport, establish some common ground, and make the individual feel welcome, which are all critical to the relationship-building process that's supposed to happen during any interview. If you move too quickly into a formal question-and-answer format, you'll likely create an expectation of formality in which candidates are hesitant to reveal their true selves. In reality, your goal should be to establish trust and allow candidates to feel comfortable sharing some vulnerability in a positive sense. Vulnerability builds trust, and your ultimate goal will be to get to know the real candidate behind all the interviewing hype.

But how do you get there? What types of questions typically make candidates feel comfortable and at ease sharing more about themselves—their short-term goals, their longer-term career objectives, and their ultimate willingness to join your organization versus the others out there that are competing for talent? Before we launch into the discussion of icebreakers and other initial interviewing queries that allow candidates to feel more comfortable discussing their wants and needs, it's important to understand how the interview should be structured. A consistent interviewing construct will ensure that you, the interviewer and talent evaluator, can focus on your keys to hire, compare apples to apples in terms of your selection criteria, and make candidates feel welcome while providing them with insights into your leadership style.

Here's a simple road map that may help you develop your own interviewing format and move seamlessly into a discussion that helps candidates assess themselves in terms of their potential fit with your organization, department, and team. After all, effective hiring always relies on the overall fit factor: the candidate's career and personal interests matching the challenges of the role you're attempting to fill. Assuming a one-hour interview, compare your current interviewing style and structure to the model that follows and see where you complement versus deviate from this typical interviewing time frame:

Step 1: Icebreaker (three minutes)

Step 2: Career interest and professional development questions (five minutes)

Step 3: Resume review: company and prior role exploration (ten minutes)

Step 4: Discipline and role-specific interviewing queries, including behavioral interviewing questions (ten minutes)

Step 5: General questions relating to fit factor, personal and career interests, and overall compatibility match (fifteen minutes)

Step 6: Counteroffer role-play (two minutes)

Step 7: Salary expectations and next steps (three minutes)— to the extent permitted under the laws of your state relative to salary-discussion restrictions before a conditional employment offer being made

Step 8: Information sharing regarding your company, role, and team, as well as challenges awaiting the new hire (ten to twenty minutes): your opportunity to talk and sell

If your typical interview only lasts thirty minutes (rather than an hour), review the percentage of time dedicated to each of the sections above to ensure that your interview is balanced appropriately.

Note that you really shouldn't begin sharing information about the company or role until step 8. Too many interviewers jump right into the company's history, its players, its historical achievements, its corporate philanthropic mission, and many other aspects of the organization or role at the very beginning of the interview, allowing candidates little input other than to nod their heads with understanding. Likewise, if the interviewer shares too much information initially about the challenges of the role, it will likely tip off candidates in terms of how they should frame their responses to the questions that follow.

Instead, in almost all cases, interviewers should follow the 80-20 rule in letting candidates talk 80 percent of the time at the beginning of the meeting. Interviewers can then share their 20 percent—opinions, words of wisdom, career advice, and the like—once the questioning is complete (around step 8).

Also, note that many interviewers begin the questioning process at step 3. They launch an interview by jumping right into technical questions about the candidate's resume without giving the individual a chance to settle in, share a bit about herself, and discuss what interested her about the role initially and why she applied. Although steps 1 and 2 combined last only five to ten minutes in most cases, they go a long way in building trust and camaraderie. Don't shortchange this critical part of the interview. Discipline yourself to reinvent your interview to focus on the candidate's interests and career needs before jumping into the technical and tactical portions of the interview.

Step 4 provides you with the opportunity to discuss discipline-specific issues with candidates to gain a sense of their depth and know-how. You'll have different sets of questions for nurses; graphics designers; HR, finance, and information technology (IT) professionals; sales and marketing associates; safety specialists; mortgage bankers; claims adjusters; and whatever other specialty roles your company hires. No book could cover all of those discipline-specific specialties, so you have the discretion at this point in the interview to ask whatever questions you feel are pertinent to the role at hand.

If you haven't discussed situation-specific questions and scenarios to ask of prospective hires, simply sit down with your boss and peers and develop a short list of questions that you all agree are important to know. After all, successful residential property appraisers may have to be willing to jump fences, climb on roofs, and face down aggressive dogs. It may sound menial or trite at first, but incorporating these types of practical and commonsense questions into your candidate analysis could go a long way in helping you identify the right fit for your organization.

INTERVIEW ICEBREAKERS TO
ESTABLISH RAPPORT AND TRUST

Once you have a structure in mind for approaching each interview, it's time to build rapport, set the mood of the meeting, and launch into some initial questions. How can you get candidates talking and fully engaged right from the start? Make candidates feel comfortable about sharing more about themselves by starting with something business related that also allows candidates to put their best foot forward, such as:

Tell me about your job search: What's motivating you to look for a new opportunity, and what have your experiences been as a candidate in the open market?

What criteria are you using in selecting your next role or company: What's really important to you at this point in your career?

Besides us, what kinds of companies are on your short list? Is there a particular size of company that appeals to you? Do you favor privately held or publicly traded organizations, or is there anything else that particularly appeals to you when considering companies where you'd like to work?

Similar questions can be asked surrounding the types of industries that may be of interest or the titles and roles that the individual may be pursuing in her current job search. Icebreakers are helpful in creating a relaxed and personalized atmosphere. People tend to be comfortable talking about themselves and their experiences without having the formal question-and-answer format coming their way right off the bat in the interview evaluation process. Openers are meant to establish the tone and tenor of the meeting, and richer discussions stem from more personalized and transparent invitations to connect on a more personal level.

If a candidate is entry level or hourly, you can adjust your opening question to build rapport and trust by asking something a bit more humorous and friendly, like:

> Most surveys will tell you that there are only two things that people hate more than interviewing: dying and paying taxes. Does that describe you fairly well, or do you actually enjoy interviewing a bit more than that?

With more senior candidates, you might want to defer to their hiring expertise or understanding of organizational design by asking questions like:

> Let me switch roles with you before we begin. When you hire people at your own company, what do you generally look for in terms of their backgrounds, experiences, and overall style? And what do you like or dislike about interviewing candidates from my side of the desk?

Explain the internal structure of your current department and where your role fits into the organization chart, including direct and dotted-line reports and immediate versus extended staff that you oversee, so that I have a contextual understanding of how your organization is set up.

Clearly, you can open with questions that reflect your style, personality, and individuality. Make the questions fairly easy to answer and inviting—the conversation will likely flow from there. What's important is that you're comfortable in your own approach and try to make the candidate feel at ease in answering questions transparently and in a spirit of healthy sharing. Too many times, employers engage in formal question-and-answer discussions without ever letting the candidate talk about their true selves. Candidates really want to know what it's like working for you. Don't underestimate the power of a strong bond or interpersonal relationship in terms of its power to serve as the ultimate swing factor in the candidate's accepting your job over someone else's.

8

THE EMOTIONALLY INTELLIGENT INTERVIEW

A "CAREER-COACHING" APPROACH TO GETTING INSIDE CANDIDATES' HEARTS AND HEADS

As mentioned, many employers jump into an interview prematurely: "Tell me about yourself . . ." followed immediately by "Give me an example of when you've . . ." With that, they're off and running into the formal question-and-answer paradigm of so many interviews. The relationship isn't quite ready for that yet. A more practical and wiser way of approaching candidates focuses on candidates' career needs and aspirations. Get them talking about themselves in light of their longer-term career planning goals, and you'll have a much more meaningful initial exchange of information—even with someone whom you're meeting for the first time.

This is a "career-coaching," emotionally intelligent approach to evaluating job applicants because it initially places their needs ahead of your own. It's a road map for building immediate rapport and goodwill and for turning interviewing into a more open and honest dialogue that focuses just as much on the candidate's needs as on the needs of your company. After all, by the time candidates come in to interview, you've already determined that they meet the technical requirements of the position you're seeking to fill. What will help you distinguish the most suitable individual for your organization will ultimately be based on a personality match, natural rapport, and a compatible business style that complement your organization's culture and unique personality.

Similar to icebreakers or your telephone screen, ask again:

Tell me again about your job search: Why are you in job search mode right now, and what's most important to you at this point in your career?

Remind me again what appealed to you when you immediately saw our job posting?

What are the two or three criteria that are most important to you at this point in your career in terms of exciting and motivating you to say yes to an employment offer?

For employed candidates who may be considering a lateral move into your organization, ask:

What would need to change at your current organization for you to consider remaining with them?

Have you openly shared your concerns with your current employer, and are they aware that you're actively interviewing? Would it surprise them to find that out?

For unemployed candidates in career transition, you might want to try questions like these:

What's been your approach to your job search up to now? How have you gone about researching the job market and what have you found?

What guidance or advice would you share with others in career transition relative to job searching in this market?

Ultimately, at some point toward the end of the interview, you might want to ask:

If you were to accept this position, how would you explain that to a prospective employer five years from now? In other words, how would this job provide a link in your future career progression?

You're asking candidates to articulate what's driving their need to change companies, what's important at this point in their career, and why your organization makes sense in terms of building their career and resume. Most candidates will appreciate your transparency.

Similar questions that might fit well, for example, might include:

What three criteria are most important to you in selecting your next opportunity?

Typically, the three most important elements when selecting a new company are the industry, company, and the people you'll be working with: Which of those three is most significant to you now?

What are the top three companies (besides us) that you would pursue right now if you could, and what position or title would you pursue in those companies?

When you researched us, what made us stand out in your mind, and what do you picture the role you're applying for looking like in an organization like ours?

Candidates may be a little thrown off by such questions because they may never have been asked to articulate those considerations to a prospective employer in such detail, but it will open the door to the bonding relationship you're looking to develop. Candidates will walk away thinking, "Wow, I've never interviewed with a company that took such a strong interest in me and my own career needs like that. They really forced me to think this move through, and if they put candidates' needs first, they probably do that for their employees as well." In short, forcing career introspection builds goodwill and trust early on. In a way, it introduces career and professional development discussions into the first interview, which is a healthy way to start any professional relationship—and set your expectations for intermittent (i.e., quarterly) performance check-ins and goal reviews. It's amazing what a difference two or three well-situated questions can do to build rapport and trust, even in a brand-new relationship. And to think you're only eight minutes into the interview!

INTERVIEWING TECHNICAL CANDIDATES WHEN YOU'RE NOT A TECHIE YOURSELF

Even self-confident managers find it daunting to interview technical candidates. It's easy to feel vulnerable when you're responsible for interviewing, recommending, or hiring technicians with expertise beyond your scope of expertise. Still, you'll probably have to do it—and make hire/no-hire recommendations or decisions at some time in your career. Here's how:

Start by stating your knowledge limitations up front and asking candidates to evaluate themselves according to their own criteria. This spares you the embarrassment of pretending that you understand the technical nature of their job and should provide you with enough information to make an evaluative recommendation based on candidates' self-analysis of their qualifications, potential or career progression, history of achievements, and shortcomings.

Let's assume you're hiring a lab technician who is responsible for gene sequencing, an important role on your team. Here's how you might start the interview:

Laura, as a business manager in this unit, I focus more of my time on the behind-the-scenes administration of the lab. I have a degree in microbiology, but I'm not as familiar with gene-sequencing techniques. I'd prefer if you answer my questions in layman's terms and teach me what you're doing by explaining it as if I've never had a day of biochemistry in my life. Would that be all right with you? [*Sure.*]

Then, ask the candidate to evaluate herself according to her own criteria. Also, ask candidates to talk about the challenges ahead in transitioning from their current companies to your organization based on differences in product lines, computer systems, research methodologies, and the like. You might follow up your initial query with a question like this:

Your current lab focuses on genome sequencing; our lab, as you know, does cancer genetics. What do you think you'd be doing differently from a gene-sequencing standpoint in our lab as opposed to what you do now in your current lab?

Then, let the candidate help you assess her technical skills. Ask:

On a scale of one to five, how do you rate yourself from a technical standpoint? If a one means you aren't very technically advanced in this particular discipline, and a five means you truly are "leading edge" technically, how would you rank yourself?

Most candidates will rank themselves as a three or a four, depending on their experience and level of comfort with the position for which they're interviewing. Few will rank themselves a five for fear of being perceived as cocky or arrogant. Once they rank themselves as a three or a four, ask:

Why would you rank yourself that way?

Then ask:

What would you add to your background to make you a five?

At that point, you'll have enough information to measure the gap between the ideal credentials and this candidate's background. Still, to help you focus further on the issue of "technical match," ask another follow-up question:

Where would we need to give you the most support, direction, and structure in your initial employment period to make sure that you excelled in this position from a technical point of view?

Likewise, why would accepting this position in our lab help you from a professional and career development standpoint? In other words, why would this be a good move in career progression in terms of building your resume and LinkedIn profile?

Armed with this information, you should be able to confidently assess the candidate and determine the degree of technical fit. Also, don't underestimate the fact that most candidates are happy to "teach" during their interview with someone who may not be as familiar with the type of work they do or their specific focus areas. Giving candidates an opportunity to explain how their role is unique and how they execute it on a day-to-day basis is healthy for them and provides you with helpful content to come to an informed decision about the individual's overall suitability.

EFFECTIVE INTERVIEW QUESTIONS FOR HIRING REMOTE STAFF

R emote employment provides greater flexibility in corporate hiring practices and workers' career management goals, but it also requires a different set of interviewing skills to find the candidates most likely to succeed remotely, when they're not working in the same office, building, or even state as you do. The general nature of working with a distributed workforce makes hiring and managing more complex and requires different sets of leadership skills and worker attributes. Other challenges and disadvantages unique to remote reporting relationships can include managers' fear that they cannot account for workers' time and efforts as well as workers' sense of isolation due to being "out of sight, out of mind." Remote employees may feel insecure and disengaged or think that their career options are limited.

Your goal in hiring remote workers is to maximize the advantages and minimize the disadvantages of the unique nature of remote working relationships. It is critical to arm yourself with sets of questions that best ferret out individuals who can thrive in this working environment.

IF CANDIDATES HAVE PRIOR REMOTE WORKING EXPERIENCE (PREFERRED)

- Have you worked in a hybrid role before, where you come to the office at specific intervals, or 100 percent remote, where you may not even have met your supervisor or coworkers in person? Which do you prefer?
- Why do you like to work remotely, and what does a successful remote-work relationship look and feel like in your experience?
- What were the specific expectations for your prior positions where you've worked remotely?
- I've found that the best remote team members are self-starters: Can you give me an example of how you typically motivate yourself to feel engaged about your work?
- In your experience, is it more difficult to feel engaged if you're remote? If so, how have you successfully overcome that?
- Have any of your peers admitted to experiencing a sense of loneliness, isolation, or disconnectedness, and how would you counsel them if they needed your help?

IF CANDIDATES HAVE NO PRIOR REMOTE WORKING EXPERIENCE (NOT PREFERRED/RISKIER)

- What do you believe are some advantages and disadvantages of a remote working relationship?
- What interests you most about working remotely?
- What are your biggest concerns about not being in the same location as your boss and peers?
- Many people don't necessarily have the organization, focus, or motivation to be productive working remotely. How do you see yourself succeeding in this if you've never done it before?

■ What do you think it takes to deliver A-level performance on a consistent basis when you're working remotely? What types of deliverables would you focus on providing?

ESTABLISHING A RHYTHM AND CADENCE OF FEEDBACK AND COMMUNICATION

■ How have you maintained a sense of community and connectedness with your manager and coworkers? Did you have virtual and in-person meetings and get-togethers at your prior companies?

■ How do you establish relationships and communication hubs with your peers to keep from feeling alienated or disconnected from the group?

■ Some leaders worry about being effective in a virtual environment because if they can't physically oversee what's happening, they can't know the work is getting done. How could you allay that concern?

■ What amount of structure, direction, and feedback do you prefer from your supervisors regarding your workload on a day-to-day basis?

■ How would you structure your communications with me to ensure that I feel confident in your work and that you will meet and exceed expectations?

SETTING EXPECTATIONS CORRECTLY AND MEASURING RESULTS

■ What kinds of measurement standards—scorecards, key performance indicators, or customer satisfaction surveys, for example—have you been accountable for in the past? Which ones work best for you?

■ Job descriptions outline what you're supposed to be doing; performance expectations outline when you're doing something well. What performance expectations have you been held to in the past, and how did you quantify your results?

■ I find that successful remote workers create goals for themselves—checklists, personal metrics dashboards, quarterly achievement calendars, and the like. What have you used in the past to gauge your performance? ([If none,] What could you see yourself creating to demonstrate your goal progression and results?)

■ In performance reviews or one-on-one feedback that you've received from past supervisors about your ability to perform and excel in a remote environment, what were your strongest attributes as well as your key areas for development?

■ What's your strategy for ensuring that your immediate supervisor never feels blindsided or out of the loop when it comes to status updates on your projects or deliverables?

■ How do you generally celebrate successes and enjoy the social elements of being part of a team when working remotely?

Aim for clarity, transparency, and overcommunication when supervising remote workers. Teamwork and operational coordination standards will likely need to be higher for them than for those whom you see and oversee on a day-to-day basis. Such flexible working arrangements can create a much bigger talent pool in which you can cast your recruiting net, giving you significant advantages and opportunities in tight labor markets. But you have to make sure that you're setting expectations clearly, insisting upon communication updates whenever there is a need to pivot or change direction, and recognizing achievements as they occur to ensure full employee engagement and satisfaction.

EFFECTIVE INTERVIEW QUESTIONS FOR HIRING FREELANCERS AND INDEPENDENT CONTRACTORS

The trend in hiring freelancers is growing significantly, and the questions suggested here should help you make stronger selection decisions when evaluating talent for these roles. In general, focus on a candidate's prequalifications, communication style and performance expectations, fee structure, and successful completion and follow-up of the work or tasks you're contracting for. This is especially important when hiring freelancers, and you should address these key issues before a consultant or freelancer begins any work for your organization.

INITIAL CONSIDERATIONS AND PREQUALIFICATION

- How much time do you have to dedicate to the demands of this project?
- In terms of the speed of your deliverables, how quickly can you produce this for us?
- Do you anticipate having any competing projects or priorities while working with us?

- Based on your understanding of our needs, how can you help our project succeed and what, if any, obstacles or roadblocks can you foresee?
- What is your general approach to launching a project in terms of strategy, effectiveness, and efficiency?
- What's the typical size of company that you support, and what niches (types of industries, nonprofit, international, startup, and so on) do you generally serve?
- Which elements from your portfolio bear closest resemblance to the project we'll need you to work on for us?

COMMUNICATION STYLE AND PERFORMANCE EXPECTATIONS

- How do you ensure that communication, collaboration, and accountability are part of the consultant-client relationship?
- If you win this project, how will you draft a road map to success? What would you do on your first day of work for us?
- What would you do if you thought you might miss a deadline? How much advance notice could we expect? Likewise, do you feel our timeline is realistic?
- How do you typically measure and communicate results, especially in terms of key performance indicators and intermittent milestones that you set for yourself?
- How would prior clients grade you in terms of your balance between quality and volume? How about your working relationships and communication style?

MEASUREMENT, ACCOUNTABILITY, AND FEE STRUCTURE

▦ Of all the projects you've worked on, which one mirrors this one most closely? What were the end results of that project, and what types of similar challenges could we expect?

▦ On a scale of one to ten, ten being the highest, how challenging is this project relative to others you've worked on? Is there any part of this project that you're not that familiar with or where you might need to rely on additional resources or subcontractors?

▦ How do you generally troubleshoot problems on your own?

▦ How do you stay on top of your work and remain committed to your project milestones?

▦ How do you structure the pricing for your services, and what is generally included or excluded from your basic fees?

▦ We'd like to speak with two or three references of yours in this space: Who would you recommend, and can you help set up the calls for us?

SUCCESSFUL COMPLETION AND FOLLOW-UP

▦ What percentage of your projects comes in on time and under budget?

▦ How would you envision the finished product if you're fully successful in this assignment?

▦ Who will own the intellectual rights to the finished product?

▦ On a scale of one to ten, ten being the highest, how interested are you in pursuing this project?

▦ How are payment installments tied to interim project completions? When is the remainder and full amount due?

Employee engagement, self-motivation, and accountability are standards that strong interviewers set for those they evaluate at all levels—whether full-time or flexible and contingent. Look for no less among those who fulfill just-in-time roles.

12

EFFECTIVE INTERVIEW QUESTIONS FOR HIRING SALES AND BUSINESS DEVELOPMENT STAFF

The sales interview is one of the most challenging, with a hefty impact on your organization's bottom line. Your task will be even fuzzier because salespeople are skilled at saying all the right things and landing on their feet in cold-call situations—which is exactly what your interview represents to them.

Because there are no clear-cut questions and answers that assess sales professionals consistently, you'll have to ask questions that will help paint a picture of the individual's manner of doing business— questions that will address drive, energy, impulsiveness, discipline, and commitment.

How do you rank competitively among other account executives in terms of your production?

Salespeople are typically bottom-line types who relish the chase of closing a deal and who measure themselves via their peer ranking. Those with the most to offer will challenge you to provide them with even greater responsibilities; the opportunities they're looking for will come in the form of stronger commission payouts or long-term management opportunities.

In comparison, those who haven't attained consistent sales often change jobs because they're not making enough money. The reason they're not more successful is typically because of their inability to establish rapport, identify a prospect's needs, distinguish features from benefits, overcome objections, or, most important, close the deal. Therefore, your mission is to locate each individual's real reason for leaving their current employer and goals for joining their next firm.

In response to this question, candidates often rank themselves according to percentages and quartiles. Obviously, those who rank at the top have no difficulty sharing those achievements with you. With these candidates, most of your interview will be spent discussing how the top producer got there, stays there, and plans to obtain the next rung on the success ladder.

But salespeople who do not reach acceptable performance benchmarks immediately volunteer reasons why their numbers were not higher. Sometimes excuses are acceptable; other times, they have little credibility. Only you know what separates excellence from mediocrity in your field. But your primary focus in dealing with individuals who rank themselves at the bottom lies in identifying the patterns for their excuses. Short-term tenures with similar types of companies usually spell inconsistent performance. In such instances, this interview question will immediately raise red flags in your mind. Proceed with caution and measure the answers that follow in this light.

What are the two most common objections you face, and how do you deal with them?

It's important to hear how a candidate rebuts common rejections, such as these:

- ▓ We don't need your product.
- ▓ We're happy with our current provider.

No matter what field you're in, these stonewalling showstoppers typically throw salespeople off. So, the first thing you want to observe is how confidently the candidate attacks the objection. Persuasion plays a big role, after all, in establishing rapport with new accounts. The second issue lies in the creativity of the individual's response. If her rebuttals sound like everyone else's, there's a chance she hasn't given much thought to what makes her product or service unique.

Therefore, beware of candidates who regurgitate hackneyed responses like these:

- ▓ I bet we could offer more competitive rates than your current provider.
- ▓ Change is good. Why not give me a chance to show you what I can do?

Such trite comebacks typically result in little new business.

Instead, look for responses that reveal creative insights and go beyond the obvious. People who leverage their backgrounds or education to a customer's advantage maintain an edge in the client-development arena. Similarly, those who put the customer before the sale build goodwill and credibility. Most salespeople do little to understand their clients' businesses, so look for candidates who do their homework and research prospects appropriately. Salespeople who present their services on a problem-to-solution level and who show patience and goodwill in the sales process turn prospects on. There's no sales pitch and, even more important, the salesperson shows a commitment to building long-term relationships. Sophisticated, relationship-driven salespeople will consistently outperform transaction-driven, buckshot types who see no farther than this month's billing log.

How would you define your closing style?

If there is one area in sales where people fail, it's their inability to persuade a prospect to take a recommended course of action. That's because closing skills really can't be taught; they stem from innate personality traits. As a result, salespeople often either (a) close prospects aggressively by repetitively asking for the sale and wearing the prospect down emotionally or (b) make a logical case for why customers would want the product and then induce customers to "close themselves."

Both styles work: there are too many fields of sales to isolate one closing style as *the* optimal manner for doing business. Although top producers usually fall into the aggressive closers group, many successful salespeople are gentle persuaders as well (especially when dealing with more sophisticated clientele). The brand of closer you want will ultimately depend on your product line and corporate culture.

Candidates typically respond that they're capable of adapting their style of closing to a prospect's needs: that's a wishy-washy response. To find out more, ask candidates to grade their closing skills on a scale of one to ten, with ten being aggressive and one being very benign.

Other questions to determine an individual's closing style include:

■ Tell me about the last difficult sales negotiation you experienced. Could your sales manager have accused you of debating with customers rather than persuading them?

■ When is the last time you chose to stick to your guns and lost a sale? How do you determine when it's prudent to walk away from a deal?

■ Realistically assessing your style, do you find that you sometimes hesitate to ask for a sale? If so, what circumstances or kinds of people hold you back?

All salespeople need to find an equilibrium between high-volume production numbers and quality. Which philosophy drives your sales style more?

Most salespeople will tell you they're basically balanced in terms of harmonizing quality and quantity. Most people, however, lean in one direction more than the other. Top producers are typically much more quantity driven. They close deals and don't look back. If they're lucky, they have a great assistant to tie up the administrative loose ends, or they do that themselves when they get around to it, but not until all the deals that could possibly close that day or month are done.

In comparison, salespeople who define themselves as more quality driven usually close fewer deals, but all the details are neatly accounted for. They take the time to follow up with customers to ensure their satisfaction. Their paperwork trails are logical and easy to follow. And they pride themselves on building a solid referral base to ensure future business. Yes, it takes longer to make the sale for these individuals, but does the smaller volume potential mean any less of a return on investment for your company over the long haul?

Only you can answer that question on the basis of your own sales style, corporate philosophy, and the amount of time you allow salespeople to show profitability. A smaller number of deals, however, doesn't necessarily equate with minimized revenues. If the profit-per-deal ratio is higher, then the number of deals closed becomes a secondary factor. Therefore, when posing this question, ask:

■ Please distinguish the *quantity* of sales from the *profitability* per sale.
■ Can you give me an example of your ability to structure high-point deals?
■ What's the size of your average sale, and how could you have gotten more mileage out of it by selling more add-on products or configuring your mark-up differently?

How many times did you fail to meet quota in the past year, and what did you do to get back on track?

Every candidate's resume will cite quotas exceeded and top production awards. But you won't find out about the hiccups in the individual's production unless you ask.

Failing to meet quota is nothing to be ashamed of: it happens to everyone—a lot. But if a candidate had four or five inadequate months in a twelve-month period, you should be concerned. Meeting quota 70 percent of the time may be a realistic expectation (although this can vary from industry to industry). Even if the candidate bills well when he's hot, too many production gaps not only will lower aggregate annual production results but may also indicate an inability to sustain performance over extended periods of time.

If the candidate responds that there were no problems making quota, follow up by asking:

How much does your production vary from month to month?

Learn about production changes that might indicate large rises and falls (even though the falls never went below the quota threshold). Finally, if a candidate provides only a vague response, ask:

How would your past supervisor at XYZ Company grade the fluctuations in your production? What would she say we could do to give you added support in that area?

Remember, asking candidates to volunteer shortcomings will provide you with a blueprint for future direction and focus.

How important is base salary to you? Would you prefer a straight commission if it offered you the potential for an additional 35 percent in aggregate earnings over the base salary?

Measuring a candidate's penchant for risk says a lot about her sales mentality. A salesperson with a husband, two children, and a mortgage may opt for a higher base pay with a lower payout potential because the timing in her life dictates conservatism over risk. If that's the reason this candidate is sitting in your office for an interview (and you happen to offer the highest base-pay program in town while all your competitors offer only straight commission), then you have lots to offer her. In this case, the problem that made her decide to leave her past company is solved by your organization.

On the other hand, if you're interviewing someone who's fresh out of college, who considers themselves a millionaire in the making, and who would opt for the $2,500-per-month base plus minimal bonus over the straight commission package, then beware: you're probably looking at an example of a risk-averse mentality, which may not thrive in a pure sales environment.

The bottom line: even if you don't offer a choice of earnings options (among base salary, commissions, and bonuses, for example), ask candidates how they'd ideally like to see their pay structured. Obviously, the higher the risk that candidates are willing to assume, the greater the aggregate payout for them.

How many prospects do you typically see before closing a sale?

Top producers focus on daily activity objectives rather than on monthly production dollars because daily activities are in their control and production results are not. Once the salesperson identifies the necessary daily activity numbers he needs to reach his production targets, question his *quality ratios*. After all, the number of outbound phone calls and face-to-face sales presentations is limited, but tighter quality ratios guarantee more results for the effort expended. Consequently, questioning a candidate regarding his activity level without balancing the equation from the perspective of quality ratios is a significant mistake that sales interviewers sometimes make.

The purpose of this question is to measure candidates' understanding of their own quality ratios and the activity numbers they need to make monthly production quotas. The most practical way to apply this question is to ask the candidate to reverse order the activities necessary to make a sale. For example, a pharmaceuticals salesperson who is expected to sell $10,000 in prosthetic devices per month might answer the question this way:

The cost of an average prosthetic device that we sell is $2,000 to $3,000. To meet my monthly quota, I need to sell four products a month, or one a week. My ratio of presentations to sales is about fifty to one, so I need to visit about ten medical offices a day in order to make fifty presentations per week and, in turn, close one sale. So, if my production ever drifts lower than it should, I make sure that I'm hitting my ten visits per day, and then I let my quality ratios take care of themselves.

Beware of candidates who have difficulty articulating their quality ratios. Without a thorough understanding of the average activities necessary to generate a sale, there's a great chance that the candidate hasn't given enough thought to his trade. If that's the case, challenge the person to calculate on the spot the numbers trail that leads to closed deals. Take notes on his out-loud calculations to ensure that his estimates (and numeric reasoning skills) are accurate. Combined with the candidate's production numbers, quality ratios will help you determine whether the individual focuses on high-payoff activities and maximizes his available time.

13

EFFECTIVE QUESTIONS TO ASK
WHEN INTERVIEWING SUPERVISORS,
MANAGERS, AND DIRECTORS

Wise companies focus on the next generation of leaders to provide them with the skills and knowledge to pick up where retiring or departing executives will leave off. This section helps you assess that next tier of talent: directors, managers, supervisors, and key individual contributors who have the potential of skilling up to become the next tier of leaders within your organization.

How would you assess your strengths and weaknesses for this position?

Beware of candidates who proclaim they have no weaknesses or are a perfect fit—they may be hiding behind delusions of grandeur or other insecurities. Likewise, they may just be snowing you. Asking candidates to objectively assess their strengths and weaknesses for a particular position is a reasonable question on your part and an opportunity for them to demonstrate objectivity and self-critical insight. Expect candidates to articulate where they are an exact match and have direct hands-on experience; they will then likely address areas where they lack experience, systems familiarity, or management oversight (for example, supervising a much larger team at your organization than they've done in the past). Whatever the case, the more objective their response, the better.

What you won't want, especially among more senior leaders or direct reports, are people telling you that they can do anything and then covering over any weaknesses or shortcomings that may make them appear to be less qualified in your eyes. Personally, I'll always side with the humbler candidate who demonstrates some level of self-deprecation in her response.

How do you measure your own progress and quantify your achievements?

Interview questions about goal setting and attainment can help you assess an individual's personal style and achievement mentality. If a candidate works for a company where formalized performance reviews and goal setting play an important role in performance assessment, simply discuss what last year's results looked like and how the individual delivered against her preset goals.

On the other hand, if the candidate's prior company didn't use formal performance evaluations or goal setting, ask the individual how she goes about doing this independently, despite the lack of formal systems or processes where she's worked. The lack of goal setting shouldn't necessarily spell disqualification, but someone who can articulate their approach to goal setting and completion may help further their candidacy in your eyes, all else being equal. Even if they don't set formal goals or have a particular answer to your question, you can still ask this:

> How have you developed a blueprint in terms of setting your own goals and guideposts for extended projects at work?

This question helps reveal an individual's approach to completing what she starts, managing through time and resource constraints, and communicating progress and roadblocks.

Are you satisfied with your career to date? What would you change if you could? Do you think you've had too many job changes or too few?

This is a good question to ask, especially if you notice short-term changes (for example, less than two years per position over the past four to eight years) that vary from their historical patterns of tenure. Of course, career changes that result from large-scale downsizings are not a candidate's fault, but it's interesting to hear candidates' accounting and reckoning of their careers in light of these current structural challenges. See whether individuals at the midpoint of their careers show anger and frustration or creativity and inspiration when they describe how they have negotiated the travails of career management at any given point in the economic cycle.

The follow-up question "What would you change if you could?" is a fair one. The invitation to look back and reevaluate the events in their education and career that have led them to this point can provide healthy insights into how they assess themselves in light of what they know now. While there's no right or wrong answer, look to distinguish between candidates who constantly look for new opportunities versus those who see themselves as victims of circumstance.

Likewise for the follow-up question "Do you think you've had too many jobs or too few?" Responses here not only shed some light on candidates' career-management values and priorities but may point to their future career aspirations. Candidates who change companies too aggressively may appear to be chasing the almighty buck rather than thinking through their career development strategically. Those who stay put without assuming greater responsibilities or demonstrating some internal career progression may lack ambition. Again, there's no right or wrong here, but addressing a candidate's career management strategies is a healthy topic for this level of hire.

Would you classify yourself as a born leader, or is leadership a muscle you've developed over time?

With this question, focus on the candidate's approach to performance, communication, and teamwork. Look for an awareness of what they feel is important regarding successful leadership. Those who have given it ample thought have likely reflected on their own strengths and areas for development in terms of visionary, transformational, or turnaround leadership as well as crisis management. Healthy leadership can show itself in any of these varying ways.

Some individuals respond to this particular question by focusing on active listening. They believe that effective leadership stems from selfless leadership or "servant leadership": people who ascribe to this philosophy put others' needs ahead of their own and expect them to respond in kind. They go out of their way to create an open and honest dialogue, base their relationships on trust, and look at leadership as a process for self-discovery. They see themselves as effective advisers, not necessarily advice givers. They're more about observation than they are about judgment, and this objectivity sets them apart. They set others up for success and then simply step out of the way. They commit themselves to helping others find their own way in an endless process of self-discovery.

Other individuals will respond to this question by distinguishing between management, leadership, and coaching. People who have this level of awareness often use terms like *engagement* and *motivation* in their responses. They strive to do their best work every day and encourage others to do the same. They demonstrate thankfulness and appreciation, which serve as cornerstones not only for their work lives but for their personal lives as well.

Look for candidates who respond to your question by making themselves somewhat vulnerable in their self-analysis. Vulnerability begets trust. Selflessness begets confidence. After all, you can't give away something that you don't already have, so leaders who *give away* time, praise, and encouragement know that they themselves possess these gifts and can give them freely to others. You'll often find candidates who respond to this question by describing their favorite boss and how they strive to be that type of leader to others.

How have you had to lead through a sudden change in plans with no blueprint to guide you?

The response you're looking for will measure a candidate's agility and adaptability. Being able to make decisions and act on them while remaining calm in the face of the unexpected is a hallmark of a strong performer and leader. The ability to adjust when facing changing circumstances amid shifting priorities is critical to any organization's success, and you're basically looking for an individual's ability to bend without breaking.

Don't be surprised if you get a response that focuses on a rare or extreme event or exception—that's how many candidates may interpret a question like this. Risk and uncertainty are the costs of doing business. Willingness to stand up and assume full responsibility for a situation gone wrong—especially where there's one with no blueprint to follow—tells you a lot about someone's self-confidence and willingness to take the bull by the horns. Likewise, an inclination to act independently versus gaining advance approval from someone else isn't necessarily right or wrong—it's strictly a matter of how you see the individual's role.

How would you describe yourself in terms of your personal brand?

Higher-level individual contributors and middle managers who are striving to increase their responsibilities in order to climb the corporate ladder often approach the concepts of conduct and results quite differently:

- Some believe productivity and results are all that count; how you get there is of secondary importance.
- Some believe fear begets respect and being too nice may be a sign of weakness.
- Others believe a healthy sense of humor and a spirit of fun and play are critical to creativity and innovation.
- Still others focus their responses on a lack of drama, always being in control of the message, and ensuring that they'll never have to ask for forgiveness because they'll always insist on gaining advance approval.

All employees—leaders and staff—are responsible for both their *performance* and their *conduct*. For example, when managers are difficult to deal with, demonstrate a poor attitude, or make others feel like they have to walk on eggshells around them, they may be performing exceptionally well individually, but they're failing in terms of their conduct. In other words, by failing to create a friendly and inclusive work environment for all, they're missing their key responsibility to the organization. That gives them an overall score of only 50 percent—a failing grade in most employers' books. In fact, asking them to grade themselves in terms of their performance versus their behavior (aka conduct) may be an interesting conversation starter. Therefore, you might ask questions like these:

▓ Where do you see yourself relative to the concepts of communication, team building, accountability, and employee engagement?

▓ Do you consider yourself a role model in terms of your leadership style, and if so, what do you do to proactively demonstrate your values?

▓ Do you find meaning in annual goal setting and quarterly update meetings with your direct reports, where you focus on their professional development and career planning?

▓ Do you ask your team members to assume responsibility for interim leadership roles or weekly staff meeting oversight?

▓ Do you support interim rotational assignments in other parts of the enterprise, so your team members gain a greater macro understanding of the business?

▓ What three adjectives would you suppose your direct reports, extended reports, and superiors use when describing your leadership style?

Inviting middle managers to assess their own strengths and weaknesses in the critical areas of behavior and conduct is often very revealing. Look not only to the philosophy behind their answers but also to the concrete examples they provide in response to your interview questions. Does their style of communication and expectations surrounding employee performance and achievement appear to match yours? Whatever their response, this question lends itself well to examining with prior superiors during a reference check.

Tell me about the difference between leadership and management in your mind.

One of the key elements of career success lies in appreciating the differences between leadership and management and between supervising and coaching. A common reason why midlevel managers don't get promoted to senior leadership is because they lack the requisite people skills.

If an individual demonstrates subpar interpersonal skills, it may likely stem from an inability to gain buy-in and trust, bond normally conflictive groups, or create trust and loyalty among peers and team members. Any of these scenarios can be career limiters. The question is always, where is this individual now in terms of his ability to forge individual bonds, grow teams, and turn around situations where employees will be expected to perform at a heightened level?

The clearest answer often reveals itself in terms of the candidate's ability to identify leadership as a behavior, not as a position. Proper leadership behavior lies in its ability to positively influence, inspire, and empower others to live the mission, vision, and values of the organization. It is a process of social influence (not authority or power), which maximizes the efforts of others toward the achievement of a goal. In contrast, leadership has little to do with management, titles, or hierarchy. In fact, the greatest leaders are often individual contributors, not responsible for "managing" anyone formally in the organization at all. In short, leadership and management are clearly not the same thing, and candidates at this level should be able to articulate their beliefs clearly.

Proven leaders or those with innate leadership abilities will often describe themselves in terms of how their actions have touched others—how they've helped others through challenges, encouraged others to get ahead, and supported others' growth and development.

They see themselves above the trenches in terms of their impact on those around them: their answers are broader and describe group and team impact rather than how matters affected only them, and they are quick to give praise and recognition for other people's contributions. While this question may appear to lend itself to a hypothetical response, it typically draws out the real core of the person in terms of how he sees himself via the relationships to those around him.

INTERVIEWING THE BOSS

QUESTIONS TO POLITELY ASSESS YOUR FUTURE MANAGER

When it comes to hiring new department heads and team supervisors, companies typically opt for one of two approaches: senior leadership either hires an external candidate without team feedback or invites staff members to meet with finalists and share input. Lower-level staff aren't typically charged with the responsibility of hiring or rejecting the candidate, since that authority rests with the senior leadership team, but their feedback is often sought as an important data point and to gain group consensus and acceptance.

When asked to participate in either a group or individual meeting with someone who's under consideration for the role of your next boss, how you approach the interview will make a lasting first impression on the candidate and provide your senior leadership team with insight into your people-discernment abilities. How can you delicately and respectfully glean important information about the individual's leadership, communication, and teambuilding styles? How do you go about asking questions that will help you come to an informed decision about what working with this individual is like in order to prepare your recommendation to your organization's senior leadership team? It's an opportunity for you to shine, both in terms of your interviewing skills and your ability to impress a future leader within your organization.

Following are some group openers that may make candidates feel at home but also let them know you've prepared adequately for this meeting and have a well-thought-out strategy for selecting candidates for this role:

> I know it's a bit awkward for us to interview our future boss, but I appreciate that our organization encourages us to do so as a team. Is this something you've done at organizations where you've worked in the past, and have you sat in our shoes in a similar situation? If so, how did you approach it?

> If you don't mind our asking, how did you find out about this opportunity, and what initially attracted you to our company?

> Most of us have been here for at least five years, so we sometimes lose sight of what's going on in the outside world. Can you share with us what criteria you're using in selecting your next position, company, or even industry, relative to what you're seeing out there in the job market these days?

Once the polite openers and inviting introductions have launched a healthy two-way conversation, it is time to get to the heart of the matter: the individual's philosophy of leadership and prior experience leading teams in similar situations.

> We prepared for this interview as a group in advance of today's meeting and determined that what keeps us happy and sticking around is

our strong sense of independence and autonomy. Have you worked with groups that have longer tenure and a fairly deep level of expertise in their field, and if so, how would you manage that type of team?

In terms of your communication style, do you tend to hold weekly staff meetings, quarterly one-on-ones, and the like, or do you tend not to schedule your meetings in such a structured way?

What's your philosophy on performance reviews? Do you love them or hate them, or are you somewhere in between? How would you advise us to make the most out of professional and career development opportunities while working for you?

Do you prefer for your team to set goals, and if so, do you measure and evaluate them on a monthly, quarterly, or annual basis? Likewise, how do you measure and track success?

What would you add or subtract to your current team (or a prior team) in order to strengthen their performance or productivity?

What's your general approach to addressing problematic performance issues? What can we expect in terms of your style when dealing with interpersonal conflict, and what's your philosophy surrounding "mistakes"?

Would you consider yourself more of a laissez-faire leader, or do you prefer providing ongoing structure, feedback, and direction? How hands-on is your leadership style?

How would you prefer that we keep you in the loop and feed information to you? Do you like informal visits in your office or being copied on emails, or would you be interested in joining us in our client meetings?

We've asked you a number of questions to get a feel for your leadership, communication, and teambuilding style. What can we answer for you in terms of our culture, our way of doing things, how we get along with one another, and the like?

Interviewing your future boss may feel a bit awkward or unnatural, but you should appreciate when your company encourages it—the request is based on trust and respect for the work you do. The candidate gets to know the team, the team members have some say over who ultimately gets selected for the role, and senior management benefits from the team's insight. It's a triple win based on trust, respect, and transparency.

CHECKING REFERENCES
AND EXTENDING THE OFFER

O nce in-person or remote interview rounds are complete, your selection process isn't over—not by half. Consider reference checks round two of the interviewing process. It's your opportunity to run your initial impressions by former supervisors who managed the individual side by side, sometimes for years. It's important to distinguish between the preoffer and postoffer steps so you're clear on the timing and rhythm of the recruitment cycle.

The *preoffer or preemployment stage* provides employers with opportunities to attract and evaluate potential talent and commonly includes the following steps:

1. Job description updates/identification of keys to hire
2. Budget approvals
3. Job postings and ad distributions
4. Telephone screening interviews
5. In-person or remote face-to-face interviews
6. Preemployment testing
7. Reference checks

8. Salary negotiations (in some states, asking for the candidate's salary history is permitted at this stage; in other states, it is not allowed)

9. Job offers and projected start dates

Once a conditional offer of employment is made, the employer then has the right to begin the *postoffer stage,* consisting of these steps:

1. Conduct background checks
2. Conduct drug screens
3. Conduct preemployment physicals

To the note above regarding salary negotiations, in some states, asking for the candidate's salary history is permitted before making a conditional employment offer. In other states, however, salary history ban laws have been passed in recent years, which prohibit employers from asking about salary history in an attempt to curtail pay disparity between the sexes. In those instances, employers are not permitted to rely on past salary information as a factor in determining whether to hire an applicant or how much to pay that person. Instead, salary offers should be set on the requirements, expectations, and qualifications of the person applying for the position rather than on the candidate's salary or prior salary history, which may reflect widespread, long-standing, gender-based wage disparities in the labor market. States handle such matters differently, which is why it's important to seek qualified legal counsel regarding your company's rights and responsibilities in this developing area.

Now let's address reference checks. You'll see that I've placed reference checks under the heading "preoffer," while many organizations conduct references at the same time as background checks in the "postoffer" stage. Here's the logic behind my recommendation: references are intended to strengthen your understanding of the individual's style of work. They provide you with an opportunity to confirm your initial impressions with a candidate's prior supervisors who can either validate or cast doubt on your initial assessment. That's why it's always better to conduct references before the offer: your goal is to match the individual's work and communication styles, work ethic, pace, time commitment, and the like to your organization's culture. Find that out before you say "I do" at the altar. It's much harder to undo an offer after the fact when you later realize you weren't happy with the reference results.

Further, references aren't necessarily designed to be good or bad, hire versus no-hire exercises: instead, reference checking helps you understand the candidate's fit factor in your organization or department. Here's an example: If you ask about an individual's ability to accept constructive criticism and find out that he can be a bit touchy and overly sensitive to corrective feedback at times, that may not matter for Hiring Manager A in your organization. But Hiring Manager B may spit fire and be known for blowing up, so hiring someone overly sensitive into that group may not make as much sense. Collecting this information up front—before extending a conditional offer of employment—makes the most sense. After all, if reference checking is the second half of the in-person interviewing process, you'll want as much information as possible up front regarding your initial insights about the candidate before extending a formal employment offer.

That being said, other organizations do indeed make employment offers "conditional upon background and reference checks." So, it's not technically "wrong" to conduct references after the offer is extended. The question remains, however, what do you do with negative reference information that you find out after the fact? The reference feedback at that point doesn't help you in your hiring and selection decision because you've already committed to the individual and leave yourself little way out if the references disappoint.

A final thought about references. Don't believe anyone who says, "References never provide negative feedback; they only give positive reviews. That's why they were chosen by the candidate." Not true! Because you're limiting your references primarily to prior immediate supervisors (versus peer or personal references, which typically only provide positive feedback), you'll often gain insightful information into a candidate's pace, autonomy, commitment level, and the like. Prior supervisors will feel challenged and engaged by the questions that follow in this chapter. Don't be surprised if some referents occasionally say, "Boy, these are great questions—I wish our company checked references this thoroughly," or "Do you have any openings there for me? I like the way you do business!" References are a collaborative effort between hiring manager/recruiter, candidate, and former supervisors. Partnering with the candidate to set up your references the right way will add untold value to your candidate evaluation and selection efforts. In short, once you realize how well this works, you'll never hire anyone again without conducting reference checks up front.

SPECIAL NOTE

When references are not available because the company is out of business, the prior supervisor can't be found, or the referent refuses to provide information beyond "dates of employment and last title held," ask candidates to provide you with copies of their prior annual performance reviews covering that time period. Unlike letters of recommendation, performance reviews typically provide positive and negative feedback and, as such, are more credible and objective documents than one-sided letters of recommendation.

True, performance reviews often suffer from "grade inflation," where superiors sugarcoat their feedback and assign higher scores than are warranted. However, when push comes to shove, documented performance reviews can provide you with similar information that you would otherwise expect to get during a reference check. As such, they help you conduct your pre-employment due diligence and gain advanced insight into at least this one employer's assessment of the employee's overall effectiveness. The point is, you have every right to ask a candidate to provide an annual performance review from a former company where the prior supervisor is no longer available to provide a reference. If the candidate doesn't have a copy of a performance review from that organization, ask her to contact the company and request copies of several reviews (the last one on file being the most important) that they can share with you, the prospective employer. It's a reasonable request on your part and an important reminder to candidates to always retain copies of prior performance reviews for situations just like this.

Finally, if the company can't provide or doesn't conduct annual performance reviews, you can then extend your review process to include key senior leaders, clients, or even subordinates. Generally speaking, you only want to speak with prior supervisors, but if none is available for a particular company and if performance reviews don't exist, speaking with other, more senior leaders who have dealt with the candidate on a dotted-line or indirect basis may then make sense. Again, you're looking for leaders who can assess the candidate's decision-making ability, productivity, leadership and communication styles, familiarity with technology, and the like. Senior-level executives from other departments or even key clients may be able to provide that critical feedback before you say "I do" to the candidate when extending an employment offer.

15

HIRING WITHOUT CHECKING REFERENCES IS LIKE HAVING A LOOSE CANNON ON THE DECK OF YOUR SHIP!

References are a critical element in the candidate-selection process. Unlike interviews, reference checks provide objective, third-party feedback of what it's like working with the candidate on a day-to-day basis. Who better than the individual's past supervisors to comment on strengths, areas for professional development, pace, interpersonal communications, and aptitudes? Indeed, making employment offers without having spoken to past supervisors is like having a loose cannon on the deck of your ship.

You also risk getting snared by the so-called *professional interviewer* who interviews much better than he or she actually performs on the job. Your candidate's past supervisors are the most qualified individuals to verify your insights into this prospective new hire's ability to make an impact on your company and to rectify, perhaps, any distorted images of the candidate's history.

Beware of past employers who refuse to comment on a candidate's performance. Human nature dictates that past supervisors will help former subordinates whom they liked find other jobs. That's even the case when company policy prohibits references to third parties regarding past employees. In contrast, when minimum-disclosure patterns begin to occur, it's sometimes because past supervisors would rather say nothing than say something negative about an employee. If you find that more than one or two former employers refuses to take your calls, or they strictly quote dates and title, proceed with caution: at best, the individual may be burning bridges; at worst, the candidate may have engaged in egregious misconduct that resulted in a summary termination or lawsuit.

You probably need no more than three references to gain insights into a candidate's relatively recent work history. Assuming the average job lasts roughly two to three years, then three references will cover ten years of work experience, and you typically wouldn't need to go back more than ten years in checking references. (That will depend, of course, on the role in question: CEOs and C-suite candidates are typically vetted much more thoroughly than earlier-career applicants.)

Never jeopardize a candidate's current position by insisting that you speak with the current supervisor prior to extending an employment offer. Candidates typically keep their job searches confidential for obvious reasons, so when it comes to checking references with current employers, show appropriate flexibility. For example, ask the candidate for two or three of the most recent performance reviews in place of a reference at their current place of employment. Unlike letters of recommendation or LinkedIn endorsements, which only show strengths and positives, performance reviews demonstrate shortcomings and areas for development as well and therefore are more objective and balanced. Likewise, consider speaking with a former supervisor from that company who's no longer there. Or else ask to speak in confidence with someone currently at the company whom the candidate trusts and who can speak to the individual's strengths, accomplishments, and areas for development without divulging the individual's job-change intentions.

Avoid speaking with peers and subordinates unless the situation calls for it (for example, if the candidate is a CEO, speaking with her subordinates as well as board of director members makes sense). Likewise, avoid personal references who can speak to the individual's character: this adds little value to the reference-checking process. After all, you'll always want to speak with former immediate supervisors who directly oversaw the candidate's work and who can share insights into the individual's style, talents, and shortcomings within the day-to-day work context. Your goal in the reference-checking process is to gain direct insights into how to provide the appropriate amount of feedback, structure, and direction to the individual on a regular and ongoing basis.

Always have candidates set up the reference-checking calls in advance with their prior supervisors rather than attempting to make cold calls. For example, if a candidate hasn't worked for a particular supervisor for three years and you make a cold call, you'll likely get hit with responses like, "All reference-checking calls must be referred to HR," or "We're only allowed to verify dates of employment and last title held." Instead, place the burden on the candidate to open up the lines of communication with the prior supervisor before you call anyone.

Falsehoods abound about references being a "waste of time" or unlawful. Further, some managers won't invest their time in checking references because "candidates only refer you to people who will say good things about them." Not true. When a candidate fills out an employment application and lists the names of prior immediate and direct supervisors, that's who you want to speak with. If your company doesn't use an employment application, ask for the names of direct supervisors during your interview and jot those names down on the resume. The focus of this exercise will always lie on former supervisors, not so much on peers or customers. Likewise, while one weak reference may not preclude someone from further consideration for an opening at your company, three poor references likely will. Running your initial interviewing impressions by two or three past supervisors can be an eye-opening experience, both to the upside as well as the downside.

Don't leave hiring up to fate:
confirm your initial impressions whenever possible.

Remember that this chapter is not a treatise aimed at addressing the legal subtleties surrounding confidential communications between employers regarding candidates' references. Nor is it a forum for discussing employee privacy rights and the potential for accusations of libel, slander, defamation, or negligent hiring. Such issues go beyond the scope of this book. But hiring based solely on an in-person or remote interview lacks historical background and depth as well as confirmation of your impressions. Further, failure to check references may give rise to negligent-hiring or negligent-retention claims should litigation arise, so refusing to check references altogether may not be a wise and appropriate policy. When in doubt, speak with qualified legal counsel about your organization's approach to this critical part of the hiring process.

16

HOW TO GET EMPLOYERS TO OPEN UP TO YOU DURING THE REFERENCE-CHECKING PROCESS

The keys to checking references in today's cautious business environment lie in (1) taking past supervisors out of the judgmental past and placing them in the evaluative future regarding a candidate's abilities and (2) removing the perception of potential liability associated with judging a past subordinate's performance and replacing it with advice on how to manage this person in order to bring out the best in his or her abilities.

First, determine, with the candidate's help, which prior supervisors you want to speak with. The more recent, the better, but you'll generally want two to three referents to speak with you that cover a decade's worth of experience. Second, ask the candidate to contact these prior direct managers in advance of your call. This way, your call won't be a surprise and they'll be more inclined to take your call and converse with you in detail. Third, ask the candidate to provide you with updated contact information and phone numbers for these individuals to maximize your time. When candidates do the legwork up front reconnecting with their prior managers and setting the stage for your reference-checking phone calls, it saves you time and provides worthwhile results. This technique is used by executive recruiters (aka headhunters) and in-house corporate recruiters at the highest levels, so adopting these practices and making them your own is a smart strategy.

When opening a conversation with a past supervisor of the employee in question, begin the call on a constructive note, which often gets people talking freely:

> Andrew, Keisha said some excellent things about your managerial abilities in terms of giving her clear direction and structure in her day. I was hoping that, reciprocally, you could share some of your insights into her ability to excel in our company.

Avoid asking generic queries right away regarding the candidate's job duties, greatest strengths, and areas for improvement. Instead, paint a picture of your corporate culture and its unique pressures so this supervisor can do some evaluative decision-making regarding the individual's "fit factor" within your organization. For example:

> We're a mortgage banking firm in an intense growth mode. The phones don't stop ringing, the paperwork is endless, and we're considering Keisha for a manager position in our customer service call center that deals with our most demanding customers. Is that an environment in which she would excel?

Assuming the employer engages in your initial question—after all, the candidate asked that former supervisor to "sponsor her" in terms of providing a reference for the opportunity at your organization— keep the conversation going on a positive note. For example:

> Keisha seems to be most interested in joining our organization because we're in an intense growth mode, and she shared that she likes

the speed and variety involved as well as the opportunity to assume greater responsibilities in a call center environment. Did she mention anything to you about this opportunity or why she's so excited about it?

At that point, you can delve into reference-checking questions like those to follow. The key will always lie in getting the prior supervisor engaged in the conversation for the candidate's sake. The questions and answers that follow should feel natural and free flowing. On the other hand, if the employer is hesitant about sharing performance feedback initially, appeal to the employer's managerial expertise:

Andrew, I won't ask you to address anything you'd rather keep confidential. We simply have several candidates in contention for the job, and we want your advice in terms of how to manage Keisha most effectively if she's ultimately selected for the job.

Because these questions focus more on future suggestions for supervision and development than do traditional queries that pass judgment on past performance, much of the stigma attached to the legal liability issues of sharing reference information will be removed.

But what if the employer still won't talk? Hard-liners who insist that corporate rules are not to be broken are the ultimate challenge in the reference-checking process. Your last-ditch strategy would be to state:

I appreciate your adherence to your corporate reference-checking guidelines. Still, I can't help but assume that no news is bad news since most employers will give a good reference to help a former worker land a new job if that person was a solid performer. My assumption at this point, therefore, is that there were likely problems with Sally's performance or conduct, which you'd rather not share. That's understandable, but again, it could really help her if you'd be willing to discuss your insights about what it's like supervising her. I'll keep what you say confidential, but it may negatively impact her candidacy if we can't develop appropriate references.

This appeal may seem like an unfair stratagem, but there's nothing to lose at this point. Besides, if the prior employer responds, "No— please don't assume that there were problems of any sort. I loved working with her, but I could lose my job if I provide references, and I hope you could respect that," then the exercise was likely still worthwhile. Andrew's defending Keisha but explaining his company's stringent reference-checking policy may certainly be reasonable under the circumstances, and it might be time to partner with Keisha to request copies of performance reviews or names of other senior leaders who may no longer be at that organization who might be willing to participate in the reference-checking process.

That being said, once you've framed your concerns so explicitly, you should rest assured that stone silence on the employer's part may represent a tacit agreement with your stated concerns. Finally, close the reference check by asking if the candidate is considered rehirable. A "no comment" response or flat-out "no" should dictate your course of action in evaluating other, more suitable, individuals.

17

EFFECTIVE REFERENCE QUESTIONS FOR NONEXEMPT, HOURLY SUPPORT/PRODUCTION STAFF

Administrative support reference questions focus primarily on superior-subordinate relationships in terms of how candidates follow instructions, work independently, respond to constructive criticism, and feed information back to you. By definition, they will differ significantly from the types of reference questions you would ask about middle managers, senior executives, sales consultants, IT professionals, and others. Take a look at some of the suggested questions below to determine what makes most sense for your organization's reference-checking exercises.

How structured an environment would you say this individual needs to reach her maximum potential?

Ask this question first when checking references because it gets former employers talking freely. Since it requires an objective response with no right or wrong answers, past employers are generally more willing to speak about future guidance issues rather than past performance problems because it places past employers in a mentoring role capable of adding valuable career advice.

Some people require fairly structured direction with lots of feedback, direction, and ongoing communication. Others work much more efficiently when their bosses simply set the parameters for a project and leave them alone to complete their work independently.

Many managers' ideal response to this question is "total independence" because they want some assurance that they won't have to babysit a demanding new employee. But the best answer simply hinges on your personal management style. If you like working fairly independently without a lot of interaction with your staff, then such a response would be great. On the other hand, if you have trouble totally letting go of projects under your control or if you enjoy mentoring and coaching new talent, you'll probably want your subordinates to keep you in the progress loop as much as possible. Therefore, you'd probably prefer working with a subordinate who enjoys ongoing direction and feedback because it keeps you tuned in to what's happening.

If you ask no other question when checking references, ask this one: it will provide you with important information about the optimal management style for a prospective new hire.

Does this individual typically adhere strictly to job duties, or does he assume responsibilities beyond the basic written job description?

As a second question out of the starting gate, this one should again prompt the past supervisor to talk openly about the candidate's work ethic. The entitlement mentality of "I'm owed a job" and "I don't do windows" is totally out of sync with today's high-demand jobs. In a radical and aggressive business environment that defines itself as streamlined, lean and mean, responsive to change, and globally competitive, increasing productivity per employee has become the key mechanism for companies to maintain a competitive edge.

This is an appropriate query for gauging administrative support candidates because it paints an immediate picture of an individual's values. One of the best pieces of feedback you'll generate will sound like this:

> The clock never stops for him. He's always looking for more things to do when things slow down in his area. More important, he has a sense of urgency and immediacy that gets things happening.

But you will sometimes receive responses that politely brush around the issue:

> Well, I can't say I really expected him to do anything above and beyond the call of duty. He does his job, and he does it well, but I wouldn't expect him to go looking for more just because it gets slow in the office.

Not every job requires a hero; some positions simply need worker bees, people who never seem to tire of the general demands of their jobs. If that's your mandate for the opening you need to fill, then don't be turned off by a response that provides little enthusiasm for a track record of assuming greater responsibilities. Workers who do their jobs well and then go home—those who work to live rather than live to work—have a place in most companies. Just be sure you're matching the right type of individual to that kind of job. Further, be sensitive to the employer's response if the candidate comes from a unionized environment, where "going beyond the scope of your job description" may be discouraged at times.

Can you comment on this person's ability to accept constructive criticism?

Oversensitivity in a subordinate is the last thing many managers want. Before asking about this, though, identify your own style of providing constructive criticism—and be honest: it might not be constructive at all. You might want to address this issue with the candidate during the interview; similarly, here's how you could explain your supervisory approach to a former employer during a reference check:

> I'm fairly direct, and I don't tend to mince words or overly concern myself about others' feelings being hurt. Can I get right to the point with Jack when there's a problem, or would he have problems working for someone who tends to have a demanding and direct communication style?

At the administrative-support level, hurt feelings and a sense of being put down and underappreciated are some of the more common reasons why employees leave companies. So don't just "wait and see"; identify a candidate's capacity for taking it on the chin before you extend a job offer.

On the other hand, if you recognize too much tolerance in your own management style and fear being taken advantage of, ask:

> I'm not an overly aggressive manager, but I don't particularly like confronting problem employees, so I try to hire very independent types who don't rely on my being present to get work done. How independently will Anthony work? How inclined is he to take advantage of another person or situation when the opportunity arises?

When your concerns are openly shared this way, you'll generate straightforward responses that provide optimal insights into managing this person.

Would you consider this individual more of a task-oriented or a project-oriented worker?

Task orientation lends itself more to the clerical-level job opening, where work instructions are dictated from above and followed rigidly. Project orientation involves much more freedom, independent decision-making, and discretion to reach targeted goals. The work mode that you desire simply depends on the amount of autonomy you want the individual to exercise in the overall decision-making process.

Past bosses typically respond to this question subjectively. If the worker exercised a fair amount of discretion on the job and was capable of moving from point A to point C while delegating someone else to tie up the loose ends at point B, he will be categorized as a project-oriented individual. Note, however, that even if the person holds the title of office manager or executive administrative assistant (titles you would expect to be more project oriented), he may be categorized as a task-oriented worker by his previous employer. Why? Because titles don't necessarily depict assertiveness, independence, or project-management orientation. Don't forget that this is a highly subjective definition.

Some administrative support employees come from environments that strongly discourage independent decision-making. Thus, they are conditioned to obtain waves of sign-offs from their supervisors before venturing into even common activities. When this is the case—even though the employee is acting according to company mandates—this individual will still be described as task oriented. This doesn't mean he couldn't handle project work independently; it's simply that he wasn't given the opportunity to exercise much discretion.

How does the candidate handle interruptions, breaks in routine, and last-minute changes?

This is the foundation of the administrative support worker in corporate America: flexibility, adaptability, and an ability to deal with last-minute change. Any kind of superior-subordinate relationship requires the subordination of one party's needs to the other's—especially in an intimate working relationship with a personal or administrative assistant. Ask this question when evaluating workers whose schedules and priorities need to mirror yours rather closely.

There are two basic ways that people coordinate the activities on their desks. Some need to complete one project and tie up all the loose ends before moving on to another task. Others pride themselves on their ability to juggle multiple tasks and keep a number of balls in the air simultaneously. Obviously, those who fit the second profile typically respond to last-minute changes more effectively than those who innately need to complete one task before moving on to another.

You might also ask the former supervisor a question along the lines of:

Maggie, my needs change on a dime, and I really would be a challenging boss if I hired someone who got flustered under pressure. How does a break in the routine throw Cole off? What's the worst scenario you could think of where he really became unwound by a last-minute change in plans or the need to pivot away from an agreed-upon course of action?

This question adds a behavioral element to your reference check in that you ask for concrete, historical evidence of how the candidate performed on the job.

How would you grade the candidate's commitment to project completion?

In most organizations, projects must be completed on time and accurately. There is simply no excuse for a mediocre work product. Project completion means follow-through in tying up loose ends and presenting a clean finished product. Most managers are big fans of daily planners and to-do lists because they represent physical proof that new information is being stored for future action. Of course, people have different capacities for staying on top of their work. But you'll most likely have more empathy for the employee who writes something down and doesn't get to it than for the worker who simply forgets details of particular assignments. If detailed follow-through is a critical skill that will separate winners from losers in your business, then ask this question to see what results you get. If a past employer says the individual's follow-through could be better, ask:

Give me an example of the types of assignments she falls down on. Are they immediate tasks that don't get done, or does Mary Jo have difficulty completing longer-term projects?

How fixable is the problem? Is it a matter of her not understanding what's expected of her? Or does she simply forget or not apply herself?

How committed is she to developing better follow-through skills?

By using these qualifying questions, you should be better prepared to dissect responses that beg for more clarity.

18

EFFECTIVE REFERENCE QUESTIONS FOR EXEMPT PROFESSIONALS AND TECHNICAL CANDIDATES

The questions in this section necessarily lack the specific details unique to your industry or discipline; only you can develop adequate questions to measure a candidate's specific performance in some areas. The key to developing such questions lies in assessing the skills that your most successful staff members have in common as well as the knockout factors that have historically made people fail at the job.

How would you grade this candidate's capacity for analytical thinking and problem solving?

It's probably uncomfortable for you to just come out and ask how smart somebody is. Still, you have a right to know whether someone is predisposed to react with emotions instead of reason. You might learn that the individual has a restless nature and is easily sidetracked, distracted, or bored. Perhaps the candidate is opinionated and argumentative, and such an inclination impedes her ability to solve problems analytically and objectively. Additionally, you may hear that the individual is overly optimistic about how quickly and easily things can be made to happen; therefore, she has difficulty saying no and spreads herself too thin and makes unduly optimistic assumptions about her subordinates' abilities without developing contingency plans.

In essence, this question demands a response to "How well does this person know her business?" This is a hands-on question regarding the candidate's ability to distinguish sound decisions from ineffective ones. And expertise in decision-making is more a function of exposure and experience than of natural intelligence. After all, no exempt professional or technical candidate will have risen through the ranks without having had his nose bloodied somewhat. And we all learn more from our mistakes than from our successes anyway.

Still, analytical thinking demands business maturity, solid listening skills, and a propensity to project the consequences of one's actions. It stems from self-confidence and awareness of personal limitations. Therefore, look out for problematic responses that point to an irrational, shoot-from-the-hip mentality, which might sound like this:

Dave is a very good underwriter, but he sometimes overcommits himself because he is overly optimistic as to what can be accomplished in a given day.

Rachel makes a fine corporate attorney, but her calling may be outside the corporate world, such as working for a nonprofit organization, and the fact that she grapples with a higher cause in all her actions can sometimes blur her ability to make effective and sound decisions.

Although Sharon is very smart, her lack of organization forces her to put out fires all the time rather than work proactively to stay ahead of problems before they surface. She doesn't always structure her plans for working through a project, which impedes her ability to solve problems effectively.

Such feedback will merit closer scrutiny as you speak with other references.

Does this individual need close supervision to excel, or does she take more of an autonomous, independent approach to her work?

Some people naturally like to work in groups, or pods, side by side with their peers. They crave recognition for a job well done, and they enjoy ongoing social interaction. For them, work is all about deriving a psychic income from developing other people's skills and abilities as they move through corporate America fulfilling their own life's agenda. These people will keep their managers in the loop regarding the status on a given project because they feel that their managers have a right to know. This way, those managers don't have to worry about the individual's performance, and there's ample reason for social interaction.

On the other side of the spectrum, you'll find the loners—the folks with a fierce level of independence who cherish the freedom to get work done their way above all else. If you oversupervise such employees, you will be accused of being a micromanager and being distrustful of them. Why else, goes their reasoning, would you need to be on top of them so much? "If you trusted me and my work, you would allow me to come to you when I had a problem." Interaction above that level is simply uncalled for.

It is ultimately your choice to hire either kind of person. Be aware, however, of hiring "loners" if you prefer to provide lots of structure, direction, and feedback on a day-to-day basis. Your natural style of management and goodwill may be perceived as burdensome to the solo flyer. In that case, recognize your own need to control situations and your preference for keeping your people on a short leash, and hire accordingly.

How global a perspective does this candidate have?
Do you see him eventually making the transition from a
tactical and operational career path to the strategic level
necessary for a career in senior management?

The ability to see beyond the immediate areas of impact and scope of responsibility helps middle managers move up through the ranks within their disciplines. It also prepares department heads to climb successfully to higher realms of corporate responsibility. Consequently, it becomes important in evaluating professional and technical candidates to measure how much the Peter Principle has played a role in their careers. The concept behind this principle is that some people have simply risen in the organization to a level where they are at maximum capacity, and this precludes their climbing any further.

There's nothing wrong with reaching such a plateau in anyone's career. After all, most people aren't cut out to be CEOs of Fortune 500 companies. As a matter of fact, you may view the Peter Principle as a practical necessity of business life that ensures continuity in the positions you're filling. After all, if you need a controller to head up a section of your accounting department, you might not really want a candidate who sees herself becoming your organization's next CFO. Not that becoming a CFO isn't a noble aspiration; it's just that it can become uncomfortable trying to placate someone who wants too much too fast. And there are few managers out there who haven't had to face that leapfrog syndrome before.

Of course, others hope to reach their first chief financial officership via a steady and planned progression through the ranks. They realize that it could take ten to twenty years in a company to reach that goal and are willing to build a list of credentials that ultimately qualifies them for such responsibility. More important, they are realistic about the time and energy commitment necessary to achieve their plan. You certainly can't take away from someone that the person is realistically building a foundation for greater responsibilities.

But what about those candidates who see themselves reaching grand career achievements but who lack the requisite talent or commitment to make that happen? That's what you want to find out via this reference-checking question.

Will this person typically assume responsibility for things gone wrong?

Most people fall into the middle of the spectrum when it comes to assuming responsibility for mistakes. At the far end of the spectrum lie the martyrs—people who take blame for everything even when they have little control or direct responsibility over the outcome. At the other extreme are the Teflon managers who are never at fault for anything; it's their supervisors, leads, technicians, and assistants who blow it all the time.

Which one bothers you more? You probably prefer the martyr to the Teflon manager: most businesspeople agree that nothing is more reprehensible than failure to assume appropriate responsibility for things gone wrong. Locating this tragic flaw in the reference-checking process is difficult. But it's pretty much impossible to find this out during an interview, and personality tests typically can't assess it; so, checking references is the only way to generate candid feedback.

You might choose to let the question stand on its own. The silence following your question can be a powerful tool that demands an honest response. A tepid and apologetic response such as this is a red flag that begs for more explanation:

Well, I don't want to say that Haley lays all the blame on everyone else, but she does have some difficulty accepting total responsibility for her team's output.

If you hear something like that, press further:

What would her subordinates say about that? Is it a matter of an overly inflated ego, or would you say that it's a fear of loss that dictates her response? Has she ever had occasion to throw a subordinate under the bus to free herself of responsibility?

This is certainly a difficult issue for employers to address. It's an ugly characteristic of what may otherwise be a successful management candidate. Still, if your previous employee (that is, the person you're replacing) tended to hedge his involvement in his unit's shortcomings, you'll want to cover this issue when checking the backgrounds of all finalist candidates.

Note that if one supervisor tips you off that this serious problem may exist, you'll want to speak with other past superiors regarding the issue. Also, you might want to conduct subordinate references, which seek to gauge the candidate's management style from the bottom up. Subordinates will typically be a lot more forthcoming in sharing information regarding a manager who places blame disproportionately on the more helpless members of the staff.

How would you describe this individual's capacity for initiative and taking action? Does he tend to get bogged down in "analysis paralysis"?

It is not uncommon for specialists in analytical disciplines to demonstrate substantial resistance to predicting final outcomes. After all, business is a practiced art of weighing risks and rewards by maximizing growth opportunities and hedging downside uncertainties. And with so much information available, making the final call can become rather difficult as mounds of contradictory evidence pile up for and against certain options.

Still, the consequences of inaction could lead to an even more significant erosion of confidence in your organization's credibility and viability. So, like it or not, analysis paralysis isn't an option, even if you're the most caring and empathetic employer in the world.

This scenario is the opposite of when candidates shoot from the hip. Just as you want to avoid those folks who play fast and loose with the facts and shoot first and ask questions later, you need to avoid those who never shoot the gun at all. The problem with the hip-shooters is that they don't thoroughly measure the consequences of their actions before taking action. The problem with the procrastinators is that they dissect the possible outcomes of their decisions to a point where they get frozen like deer in an oncoming car's headlights. Not always, of course, but in enough situations (or in one critical instance) to make the former supervisor label the individual as gun-shy when the heat is on.

If you receive a benign response that a candidate never shoots without aiming and equally has no problem making the tough calls, then conclude that this issue will not adversely affect her performance. On the other hand, if her past employer raises serious issues regarding the candidate's tendency to leap without looking or to freeze up from the pressures of taking definitive action after analyzing complex information, then reexamine the individual's candidacy. If your style will temper the individual's approach toward decision-making, then your being forewarned will put you in a better position to provide added support immediately. If not, realize that your decision-making styles may be incompatible and move on to your next candidate.

19

EFFECTIVE REFERENCE QUESTIONS FOR REMOTE HIRES

Remote hiring and the hybrid workforce model have been coming of age since the enormous technology gains of the early twenty-first century have taken hold. But nothing could have prepared us for the exponential changes that came about after the COVID-19 pandemic in the early 2020s. New skills, knowledge, and abilities were sought after, as an independent workforce came onto the scene en masse, untethered to the traditional in-person nine-to-five routine that has marked the global workforce since the Industrial Revolution. True, the expansion of global work varies depending on industry (manufacturing versus service), worker level (exempt versus nonexempt), familiarity with technology, and corporate cultures. Whatever the case, being prepared to hire remote workers at any given time is a critical skill in your tool kit, so let's look at key issues to ask of prior supervisors during reference checks.

Note that the questions below can be altered, depending on whether the candidate has prior remote work experience or if this is the first time the individual would be working remotely. Further, these questions can be added to any of the other reference questions that you typically ask to capture this remote element of the individual's performance. Notice as well how closely these questions tie to the interviewing questions in topic 10, "Effective Interview Questions for Hiring Remote Staff." After all, interview questions lead naturally to reference queries so that you can test your impressions of a candidate's responses with prior supervisors who have experience working with the candidate under just those circumstances.

The following reference-checking questions should go a long way in opening up a realistic dialogue with prior supervisors. Choose the questions that fit your scenario best, and either make these questions the core focus of your reference check or add some of these questions to the standard questions that you already ask:

How well did Damian perform in a distributed workforce model? In other words, when you think about the various aspects of a remote worker—independence, upward communication skills, time management, and a project completion and goal-setting focus—how well did he perform as a remote contributor?

[*Optional*] Many people don't necessarily have the organization, focus, or motivation to be productive working remotely. Can you see Damian succeeding in a remote role if he's never done this before?

Was he working more in a hybrid model, where he came into the office at specific intervals, or was he 100 percent remote? [Which model worked better for him?]

How did Damian typically keep you in the loop in terms of progress toward his project goals? [Was it too much, not enough, or just the right amount of feedback and communication as far as you were concerned?]

In terms of remote teambuilding and a sense of camaraderie with his peers, was Damian a strong contributor to team goodwill? Was he able to express his true personality despite the limitations of working remotely?

Did the natural flexibility inherent in a remote working relationship work to Damian's advantage? In other words, did he stand out as a rarity among his peers in any way because of the remote working relationship, or do you feel he would have performed at a higher level had he worked on-site?

How confident were you that you could account for his work and whereabouts at all times? Did you ever feel like you were flying blind in terms of his availability and commitment, or did it always feel "tight" in terms of your knowing that he was "on it" at all times?

Is Damian a natural self-starter who finds ways of motivating and challenging himself, or do you find that he generally needs more specific direction and feedback? [Was it an appropriate balance in your opinion, or did you find that he needed a lot more structure than you would have otherwise expected?]

In general, was Damian able to produce deliverables consistently and on time? [How often did you find that you needed to adjust deadlines in terms of his project completions?]

I find that successful remote workers tend to create goals for themselves— checklists, personal metrics dashboards, quarterly achievement calendars, and the like. Does Damian tend to use tools like these? If not, how does he generally demonstrate goal progression and results?

How has Damian maintained a sense of community and connected-ness with his coworkers and peers? Did he contribute during virtual staff meetings and online get-togethers? How did he establish relationships and communication hubs with his peers to keep from feeling alienated or disconnected from the group?

Back-to-back remote meetings can easily start to feel transactional after a while. Was Damian able to inject his personality into his meetings and bond with customers and coworkers, despite not being with them there in person?

[*Optional*] How much impact did the time difference have between your offices? Was he able to accommodate your/corporate's schedule despite living two time zones away? Did his scheduling flexibility ever become a point of concern for you?

Sometimes, remote workers sense isolation or fear that they're "out of sight, out of mind" in terms of gaining healthy exposure to other leaders or the company as a whole. Did Damian ever express concern about his lack of visibility to corporate or a sense of loneliness or isolation that can come from a remote working relationship?

Did you ever experience any disadvantages in terms of Damian's working remotely that likely wouldn't have been a problem had he worked on-site?

How would you grade him overall, relative to being an effective remote contributor, on a scale of one to ten (with ten being highest)?

Would you rehire Damian into a remote position if you had the opportunity? [Would you rehire him in general, remote or on-site?]

The biggest challenges surrounding remote work will continue to be communication, collaboration, inclusiveness, and culture. Craft reference-checking questions that address these four key challenges and apply them consistently to increase the likelihood of hiring remote workers that fit into your organization's culture and provide you with enough information and feedback to feel confident about the individual's commitment and performance.

20

PREEMPTING THE COUNTEROFFER

SETTING THE STAGE FOR THE EMPLOYMENT OFFER

Counteroffers are simply enticements to keep employees aboard once they have given notice. Employers have historically been known to appeal to a departing worker's sense of loyalty, guilt, or fear of change to convince individuals to rethink their decisions to resign. It is not even uncommon to hear of offers of promotions, huge salary increases, and spousal perks to entice resigning employees to reject a new employer's offer.

It may seem more logical to handle counteroffer issues with candidates *after* they've accepted your job offer. After all, most employers reason that they have to offer someone a job before the candidate will receive a counteroffer. But it's critical to address counteroffer issues *before* extending an employment offer. Once you make an employment offer, you give total control over to the candidate. The individual then could very well use the counteroffer threat as leverage to negotiate more money from the current employer. Remember, the counteroffer is just another variable in the employment process that you need to control.

What should you do if a candidate intimates that he'll consider a counteroffer from his present employer? Simply advise him to address his needs with his boss right now: this will proactively remove an arrow from the candidate's quiver that could have come back to hurt you later in the negotiation process.

This section addresses how to preempt counteroffers. Preempting the counteroffer in a conversation that leads up to a formal job offer is sometimes known as a "resignation drill." Resignation drills occur often in the recruitment industry when headhunters take their candidates through role-play scenarios of giving notice to the current boss. It makes sense for recruiters to spend some time preparing the candidate to resign so as to avoid surprises at the finish line that could wipe out all the work that has gone into the negotiations up to that point. So, it's practical business sense that leads recruiters down this path. Resignation drills will benefit you as well as the hiring manager by dramatically increasing the chances that candidates will accept your employment offer and make a clean break from their current companies.

Tell me again why you feel the position you're applying for meets your career needs or why working for our company is so important to you at this point in your career.

This question helps you mentally prepare the candidate to accept your offer. The counteroffer prep and resignation drill function as a preclosing technique to ensure that the candidate is aware that he may be propositioned once he returns to his current office to give notice. Therefore, the initial step in the process will require that the candidate voice out loud what benefits he'll gain by joining your company. This is specifically done by having him focus on how his personal or career needs are linked to the opportunity that your organization offers.

Candidates typically join companies for one of three reasons: the company, the position, or the people. Candidates must convince you and themselves that their reason for leaving their present employer can be fulfilled by joining your company. Don't assume that the benefits and the appeal of your organization are obvious to an outsider.

On a scale of one to ten—with ten being you're really excited about accepting our offer and one meaning you have no interest—where do you stand?

This follow-up question forces candidates to come to terms with their own emotions and motives for job change as well as to volunteer any concerns they have about accepting your offer. If you ask a candidate where she falls on a scale of one to ten and she responds that she's an absolute ten, that's great. But beware: these are relative numbers, and it's the reasoning behind the numbers that counts, not the numbers themselves. For example, if Laura says she's a ten, your immediate comeback is, "Well, that's excellent, Laura. I'm happy to hear that. What makes you a ten?"

By qualifying the number, the candidate is forced to articulate her definition of a ten. If Laura is a ten because she's currently a management consultant for a Big Four accounting firm who wants to move into her first in-house controllership, then your offer makes solid business sense for both of you. The chances of her rejecting this offer are slim.

If, on the other hand, she's a ten because she's having difficulties getting along with her fickle boss, then she may be a fake ten. Interpersonal relationships change quickly with erratic supervisors, so that one day you're in and the next day you're out. Consequently, if the two work out their differences, or that boss leaves the company, then your motivated ten candidate might succumb to a counteroffer anyway. Beware the jilted subordinate.

Let's say, however, that Laura answers that she's an eight. In that case, you need to find out why she's not completely enthusiastic about your job offer. Find out why she's an eight and what would make her a ten. Once you've discovered her objection, you can "pre-close" her to accept your offer if you can address and overcome the gap she described.

What would have to change at your present position for you to continue working there?

Whenever you're dealing with someone who's doing excellent work for a competing company, spend some time analyzing what's going on in the person's current position so you understand how your offer stacks up against it. (Of course, if a candidate is currently unemployed, this question is irrelevant.)

When asking this question, look first for responses that are out of the individual's control. Pending layoffs, corporate relocations, and overall job insecurity will often result in the candidate responding, "Paul, nothing could change at my present company to entice me to stay." That points to a clean break with the current employer and a graceful transition into your firm.

In contrast, if the candidate responds vaguely, "Well, I can't really think of anything offhand that might change at my present company and convince me to stay," then challenge her again by stating:

> I've found that one or two changes could often make an individual think twice about leaving a company. What would those one or two areas be in your case?

If that query still generates only a superficial or vague response, probe even deeper:

Do you feel your contributions are properly recognized, or are they somehow diminished by your current supervisor?

You're obviously leading the candidate down the path of coworker relationships. For the noncommittal candidate who is reluctant to address any shortcomings about her present company lest she weaken her negotiation posture, or for someone who hasn't given much thought to fixing relationship problems back at the office, this questioning pattern should force a critical issue to a head. After all, there is likely a weak link somewhere in the chain that binds the candidate to her present company, and statistically, there is an excellent chance that it stems from an interpersonal challenge with her boss.

Even if the candidate feels she's properly recognized for her efforts, this add-on question regarding the individual's relationship with her boss will naturally segue into other reasons for leaving:

No, my relationship with my boss is fine. However, the company lacks state-of-the-art systems that would allow me to stay on top of the power curve in my field. Also, they brought in a new CEO about four months ago who's really changed the way things are done back at the office. All in all, I feel it's the right time for me to explore other career options and make a change.

Bravo. You've brought this issue to a logical conclusion and mandated that the candidate voice out loud that her current situation is most likely beyond repair. That's an important psychological step to prepare the person to make the break. It also allows you to further understand how you should position your offer once the time comes.

Tell me about the counteroffer your company will make you once you give notice. If you gave notice right now, what would your boss say to keep you?

This question mentally prepares the individual to deal with the counteroffer awaiting her. This way, when it comes, it won't be a surprise that catches her off guard or otherwise lets her emotions cloud her better business judgment. On the other hand, if her company makes no counteroffer when she's expecting one, she'll likely feel somewhat let down by her current employer and feel even more strongly that the career change makes sense at this point.

Preparing for a concrete challenge to your potential offer makes practical sense and allows you to take sides with that individual by working together to plan her resignation and her successful exit out of her current company. A psychological good guy/bad guy contrast forms in the candidate's mind, with her current boss playing the potential bad guy who is out to tempt her with perks that will only stand in the way of her succeeding at a new opportunity. Forewarned is forearmed for candidates, too, and this brief exercise removes a snare that could entrap them.

If you sense some danger in the candidate's response, revealing that a hefty counteroffer will be made or that it will be particularly difficult for the individual to break the personal ties to her boss, follow up this question by asking:

What would change in your present position if you *did* accept a counteroffer? Would life six months down the road be any different than it is right now? Would you excel there as you could here?

By allowing the candidate to play out this scenario in her head, you'll take her past the immediacy of the resignation counteroffer and further into the future. Statistics bear out a bleak reality for those who accept counteroffers—most are gone within six months, having lost the immediate opportunity at hand to grow and develop their careers—but you can't necessarily say that to the candidate, because you're a biased party in this negotiation. But by pointing the candidate in this future direction, you're allowing her to reach the same conclusions about the limitations of staying with the current employer.

As a prospective employer, you are perfectly within your rights to find out what could entice the individual to stay with her current firm. That's not being nosy, and it's an effective way to gauge a candidate's true interest level. After all, you have the job opportunity to offer. No matter how tight the labor market or how specialized a candidate's skills, one law will always remain firm in the land of employment hiring: the employer decides who gets to join the team. Use that guaranteed leverage to drill finalist candidates regarding their interest level in your company, their potential to accept a counteroffer, and their overall desire to make a positive impact on your organization. You'll simultaneously help them avoid becoming a victim to the dangers of counteroffer syndrome.

21

SALARY NEGOTIATIONS DONE RIGHT
MAKING THE OFFER AND CLOSING THE DEAL

O nce you've concluded your interviewing process, you should "pre-close" your chosen candidates so they will want to accept your job offer. The worst time for them to be examining the pros and cons of leaving one company and joining another is now—at the actual time of the offer. Emotions run high at the finish line, and if they haven't played out this final scenario in their minds up until now, they may fall victim to counteroffer temptation.

Of course, as the employer, you don't want to have to convince someone to come to work for you. If it's that much of a challenge just to get the prospective new hire to say yes to an offer, then this is probably a premature decision on the individual's part.

Don't underestimate the tremendous pressure that most people feel while undergoing this significant rite of passage. Job change ranks right up there with fear of public speaking and fear of death in terms of causing anxiety in most of us humans. And rightfully so: severing the ties with a job where you know exactly what is expected of you, with your corporate family, the familiar restaurants where you have lunch, and the comfortable chair that you've broken in to fit your back conjures up intense fears in even the most confident people:

What if the new company experiences an unforeseen layoff? At least here I've got tenure and would probably survive the first few rounds of cuts. I've heard a lot about people getting axed because of LIFO: last in, first out means I'd be the first one out on the street. Is my present job really so bad?

Empathy for the job changer in the final decision process is crucial because while the new opportunity is exciting on the one hand, it requires disloyalty to the current employer on the other. Therefore, make your offer from a pull-sell rather than push-sell standpoint, and ask the questions discussed in this section to make the candidate pursue you rather than vice versa.

What's changed since the last time we spoke?

If there is a change in plans on the candidate's part at the time you are about to extend an offer, now is the opportunity to share that with you. The last thing you want to do is make an offer only to have it put on hold because of unforeseen circumstances.

Nine times out of ten, the candidate will respond that nothing has changed. In that case, you have the green light to move forward with the offer as outlined below. On the other hand, if something has changed—such as a sudden increase in responsibilities at the present company, a significant raise, or another job offer, or if the idea of relocating suddenly loses its appeal—then you're pushed back a step to the information-gathering stage that occurs in the counteroffer role-play. Find out what's changed, where the candidate stands on a scale of one to ten in terms of his interest in the position, and then go back to the drawing board to see if there is anything you could offer to fix the problem.

Beware of candidates who suddenly request long time frames to come to a decision. Ideally, the candidate will have had enough opportunity during the multiple rounds of interviews to research your organization, speak with the key players at your company, and accept your employment offer on the spot.

Candidates who request an additional week or more are usually waiting to hear from a different company about another pending offer. Putting you off is the only way to buy time to see whether they can generate the offer they *really* want. This is unfortunate timing for you because you're the backup job offer. Statistically, the chance of having your offer accepted, even if the individual's primary job doesn't come through, is marginal at best. People who tie their hopes to one job that ends up falling through usually decline the secondary job offer and simply restart their job search.

If you suspect that a candidate is stonewalling you in an attempt to wait for another offer, communicate your perceptions openly. Ask your candidate:

What's holding you back from saying yes to our offer?

If your perceptions are correct, the candidate will admire your intuition and respond to your legitimate concerns. You'll learn what your chances are of landing this individual, and you can prepare either to wait out his decision or to line up other candidates.

What you don't want to do is attempt to convince the candidate at the finish line that your offer is superior. His focus is definitely on the other offer—otherwise, you would have heard an "I'll accept" already. So, trying to convince him that you're better than his other suitor puts you at a disadvantage in the negotiation process: it will appear that you're begging as you shoot down the other company or try to resell your own. Again, by now, you've done all the selling you need to do. Make a firm commitment to your own plan of action and respect the individual's right to plan his own destiny.

If you had to choose among three factors— (1) the company, (2) the position you're applying for, or (3) the people you'd be working with—which would you say plays the most significant role in your decision to accept our offer?

You want to make sure this candidate has a clear understanding of what your organization is all about. He needs to hear again *out loud* what benefits and opportunities exist by joining your firm.

You'll find that most people choose option 1—the company—as the key reason why they change jobs. People look for the emotional recognition of a job well done, they want to work for a company that takes care of its people, and they want to know they can make a difference. Those emotional criteria are inherently found in the company and all of its manifestations: its people, its corporate culture, and its mission.

Don't be surprised, however, to find administrative support candidates linking themselves to option 3. Workers who define themselves by the relationships they keep often see themselves via the people they report to. So, an executive assistant reporting to a chief operating officer will probably base more of the decision to accept your offer on the perceived relationship with the COO. Likewise, bench scientists often leave one university, laboratory, or hospital to join the team of a principal investigator whom they've been following all of their careers.

Similarly, some aggressive corporate-ladder climbers may be more motivated by the increased responsibilities that the new position offers or the advanced technology systems that your organization employs. The enticements of a greater span of control, budgetary responsibilities, or exposure to new areas of interest increase the individual's overall marketability (option 2).

In short, any of these answers is fine. What's important is that you understand the key drivers that are motivating candidates to break ranks with their current employers and transition over to your team. That emotional connection will serve as the glue that binds the new hire to your organization for at least the first year. Beyond that, it's the hiring manager's and department's responsibility to create an environment in which the individual can thrive, motivate herself, and find new ways of adding value, both to the organization and to her resume.

What final questions can I answer to help you come to an informed career decision?

This is the final setup before the salary negotiation. It gives you a chance to show yourself as a concerned and empathetic future employer. Such consideration will no doubt be very welcome to all candidates about to make a break with one company and commit to another. As such, this benevolent approach should be assumed in all final negotiations. More important, it invites airing of any issues or concerns that could botch the acceptance of the offer.

If any issues other than salary beg for more consideration on the candidate's part, then go back to the drawing board and handle those concerns first before moving on to the final and most critical element of all: making the salary offer.

Candidates will typically ask for confirmations about the job responsibilities, reporting relationships, or benefits packages. Sometimes they'll mention that they have a two-week vacation already planned that can't be canceled and would like that time off without pay. Maybe they'll need to give three weeks' notice instead of two. Now is the time for such incidentals to surface.

What shouldn't occur, though, is that the candidate's demands suddenly skyrocket. For example, if an individual states that he forgot to tell you he has $25,000 worth of stock options that he expects you to include in his base salary, that smacks of extortion. Such take-it-or-leave-it propositions at the finish line are the ultimate show of poor negotiation timing. Be very leery of going ahead with an offer when such leveraging occurs in the eleventh hour.

The following can be explained either by the HR recruiter or by the hiring manager, depending on how your company handles job offers:

Jacqueline, before we discuss a specific salary offer, I'd like you to know how we develop them. We look at three things in determining a new hire's starting salary: salary range, budget, and internal equity. Let me explain how they all work.

1. The salary range is the full rate of pay established for a particular position. The spread can be quite broad—oftentimes approaching 60 percent from the minimum to maximum—and a salary range is assigned to each position in our organization.

2. The budget is typically a set dollar point that the company has factored into backfilling the role. It represents the maximum that the company would ideally like to pay, all things being equal.

3. And internal equity is the most important concept: we slot a new hire's years of experience and skills and education into that of our existing team. It's the most logical way to ensure fair pay and the integrity of our compensation program because the compensation of the entire group has to remain aligned.

[But what I'd like you to understand up front, Jacqueline, is that the offer we place on the table isn't a starting point for negotiations:

that's not how we do this. Instead, it's the best offer we can make without violating the internal equity rules. If you feel the offer is fair and accept it, that's great. If you're not able to accept it, however, we likely won't be able to increase it. Does that sound reasonable to you in terms of our approach?] [*Yes.*]

OPTION A:

Okay, then, based on our discussions up to now and your interviews with our team, what do you believe would be a fair offer in light of the position you're considering with us?

OPTION B:

Good news: we'd like to move ahead with an offer. In your case, Jacqueline, we slotted your years of experience, education, and skills against that our of existing team, and the salary offer that would make the most sense to us is $65,500. We feel that's a fair offer relative to the external market, and it represents a 15 percent increase over your current salary at XYZ Corporation. We'd like to congratulate you and confirm a start date, but what are your thoughts at this point?

The paragraph in brackets above option A may make sense if you truly have a limit to the offer you can extend. Under such circumstances, state that up front so the candidate doesn't assume that whatever offer you initially propose is "open to further negotiation." It's fair, it's respectful, and it indicates that there likely won't be much in terms of further considerations once you place your offer on the table.

Option A (which allows the candidate to propose a salary for the position in question) may make sense when you're dealing with a newly created job or the candidate's current salary is higher than the position you're attempting to fill. For example, if you know your company pay for this position is light relative to the external market, and the candidate you're interviewing was a manager in her last role but is willing to accept a senior analyst position at your firm for whatever reason, you might ask the candidate to proffer an initial number. Logically, she knows that it will represent a cut in pay, but the degree of the cut may be up for debate. This works well when you've got the flexibility to increase the offer if need be.

Option B (which states the offer up front and leaves it at that) may make sense when you can't go any higher for budget or internal equity reasons. Simply let the candidate know you're offering the top dollar that your compensation system will allow and see how the individual responds. There will be times when you simply can't afford a particular candidate no matter how much you like her. In practice, that typically reveals itself before you get to the offer stage, but at times, you won't know until you put a firm offer on the table. If a small amount may make the difference between a yes or no response, it may be worth revisiting the matter with your boss or compensation committee to ask for an exception. And yes, it can be frustrating to lose someone at the finish line for compensation reasons. What's best is if you're fair and transparent all along. Then you simply have to let the chips fall where they may and respect the candidate's ultimate decision.

Salary offers are typically not a total surprise because somewhere along the line—whether during the initial telephone screen or somewhere during the initial rounds of in-person interviews—the topic comes up. After all, no one—neither employer nor candidate—wants to invest time and energy into pursuing an employment offer that neither side can afford. Still, option A is certainly a softer and more engaging approach, whereas option B basically shuts the door as soon as it's opened. Discuss which option lends itself more to your culture, business, and communication style.

SPECIAL NOTE REGARDING
ALLOWING FOR BUYER'S REMORSE

Candidates who accept job offers often become susceptible to counteroffers at their current organizations. That's why we cover "preempting the counteroffer" before actually extending an offer of employment. Still, feelings of fear and guilt sometimes creep in after the fact: "What if I don't like it there? At least I know where I stand at my current company. I'm going to really miss having a coffee shop in the lobby of our building when I need to get away for a break. And it's killing me to leave the friends I've made here at my current company: they all want me to stay."

Such feelings are normal and common in almost all cases. Sometimes, however, they can weigh enough on a candidate's mind to either rescind their resignation at their current place of employment or fail to show up on the first day at your company. That's especially true when the current employer engages in counteroffer discussions that may result in increases in pay or promotion.

The best solution is to remain in contact with the new hire during the two-week-notice period. Consider inviting the individual to lunch—whether in person or remote—or inviting her to a company meeting or event where she'll have an opportunity to meet her new teammates. Keep things exciting by remaining in touch. The "out-of-sight-out-of-mind" approach where you assume that she'll simply show up in a few weeks may disappoint you if you leave it all up to fate. Show your support early on and through and through. Until that person is sitting in her seat in your office, there are no guarantees that she'll actually start with your firm and resist the temptation to remain with her former employer.

PART

4

ONBOARDING

Many companies spend significant amounts of time sourcing and attracting candidates, interviewing them and checking their references, doing background checks and drug screening, but when the candidates show up for the first day of work, companies often underwhelm them. Few organizations dedicate appropriate resources to the overall onboarding experience, which, unlike the new employee orientation (NEO) that takes place on the first day, should occur over the first one to three months, with a six-month follow-up for good measure.

This chapter describes what I believe a company should do to maximize the success of new employees on their first day of employment; at the end of the first, second, and third month on the job, and when they've completed their first year with your organization. Check-ins at appropriate intervals asking for personalized feedback go a long way in strengthening relationships, demonstrating respect, and building trust.

And once the initial ninety-day program is complete, you have the opportunity to establish go-forward expectations about quarterly check-ins that new hires are responsible for scheduling and managing, placing you into the role of coach and mentor throughout the performance year. It's a simple exercise in delegation that treats team members like adults and helps them quantify their quarterly achievements for you, keeping you abreast of any roadblocks coming their way or pointing to any pivots you'll likely need to make. Best of all, it's all up to your new hires to manage: you simply have to establish your expectations up front and get out of the way. That's smart leadership any way you look at it.

22

ONBOARDING DAY ONE

WELCOME ABOARD

Many companies do little more than new employee orientation (NEO) on a new hire's first day. Some dedicate a full day to NEO, while others try to limit it to a half day or even to one hour. That's a critical oversight on their part. Transitioning new hires into your company has multiple cascading events that take place over time—for the leader, the new hire, and the organization. Much more than merely enrolling people in benefits and setting up their payroll, it's your first chance to make a good impression and truly integrate the individual into your culture. This section discusses various aspects of onboarding to ensure that your investment in your new hires is well spent and appropriately planned.

While NEO typically introduces new hires to company policies, codes of conduct, safety requirements, organization charts, and the names of key leaders within the organization, the onboarding process provides you with an opportunity to orient new hires to ensure maximum engagement and productivity right from the start. On a very broad level, onboarding provides you with an opportunity to do the following:

1. *Explain what your organization emphasizes and values.* These issues need to be clearly demonstrated over time because they define your company at its core and clarify what differentiates your organization from your competition.

2. *Create "true believers" and sell your company's story while highlighting its history and achievements.* Not everyone needs to understand your company's financial statements and SWOT (strengths, weaknesses, opportunities, and threats) analysis, but all new hires should understand what your company does, how it does it, and what it wants for its employees. This is a special opportunity to sell your organization's uniqueness, and trying to unload everything in one day will surely miss the mark in helping your new employee appreciate and value your culture and heritage.

3. *Set expectations regarding the customer service experience.* What is it that you expect from your new hires in terms of servicing both internal and external customers and clients? What are your rules of engagement so that everyone knows what you value and what you model? Some companies give new employees a brief handout that explains their expectations.

4. *Set appropriate standards for how you want new hires to value their work and see their connection to the bigger picture.* As the Walt Disney Company aptly puts it, do you teach your employees to lay bricks or build cathedrals? Do your employees understand their connection to the broader picture? Do they know why and how the founders created the organization? Do they recognize the value your organization brings to its customer base and the community overall?

5. *Explain that a new hire's performance is reviewed at ninety days, six months, and one year, and that merit increases occur at the time of the annual performance review (or whatever cycle your*

organization follows). New hires can use these review opportunities to better understand where they are now, where they want to be, and how to get there. Explain how performance review templates, goal-setting worksheets, and self-review forms are used, as well as individual development plan (IDP) templates to help employees set their sights on longer-term achievements and goals right from the start.

How you handle the employee's first hour, first day, first week, and first three months on the job provides you with multiple opportunities for contact, feedback, suggestions, and clarifications. Compared to the "sink or swim" onboarding method used by many companies during NEO, this strategic approach to new-hire onboarding will drastically increase your chances of success and long-term retention.

Assign a mentor to the new employee. Weekly one-on-one meetings with a mentor or ambassador on the same team can provide a terrific return on investment for both the mentor and the new hire. New employees appreciate having someone to guide them through the ins and outs of the organization and the hidden "land mines" that could otherwise derail an early career, and to be a resource to help them get to know the players and their personalities and penchants that much better. Such relationships build trust and camaraderie, but more than that, they help new hires integrate into your company with more confidence because of the safety net they provide.

And what a great stretch assignment for more senior or tenured team members! Placing people into leadership roles on an intermittent basis increases their sense of self-worth. It provides them the opportunity to grow and develop new team members—a great strength to add to someone's personal brand and reputation. And it provides a healthy sense of competition in which the more senior team member has skin in the game to ensure that the new hire is successful. In fact, some organizations make new-hire mentoring and ambassadorship an initial requirement for anyone looking to be considered for nomination into the company's "high-potential" program. These are all important elements of a healthy working environment that focuses on employee growth and development, while capitalizing on the organization's investment in the new hire.

23

ONBOARDING DAY THIRTY

INITIAL IMPRESSIONS AND "FEED FORWARD"

A thirty-day sit-down review is an excellent opportunity to check in formally and see how the new hire is progressing. In fact, new-hire turnover within the first thirty days isn't at all uncommon. It's actually a key area of vulnerability as people transition into your organization, so having a plan to sit down with them one-on-one and review their experiences is a smart investment of your time. It will logically help you course correct if anything was miscommunicated in the hiring process (especially in terms of roles and responsibilities) or remove roadblocks that may have popped up early on in the new working relationship.

This private sit-down meeting should occur no matter how much you interact with the new hire on a day-to-day basis. That's because the questions you'll discuss are about the new hire, his experiences with the onboarding process, new questions he has that require deeper explanation, his opportunity to share who's been exceptionally helpful to him, and his overall impression with the culture and working environment. Those types of topics don't come up in normal everyday conversations. To assume that you "know exactly how the new hire feels" by your day-to-day interactions will likely miss the point: dedicated one-on-one time is always appreciated by new hires. It feels special. It means a lot. Even if the meeting only lasts ten or twenty minutes, it's an excellent investment of your time.

The challenge most hiring managers have in conducting such meetings is that they don't know what to ask. Following are some suggestions to get your conversation started and ensure that the new hire's trajectory is on target and going as planned.

THIRTY-DAY ONE-ON-ONE FOLLOW-UP QUESTIONS

Why do you think we selected you for this position?

What do you like about the job and the organization so far? What's been going well? What are the highlights of your experiences so far? Why?

Tell me what you don't understand about your job or about our organization now that you've had a month to roll up your sleeves and get your hands dirty.

Have you faced any surprises since joining us?

What one thing stands out to you the most in terms of capturing your first full month with us?

What can I help with? Can I support you with anything at this point to help you continue to onboard and integrate into our organization more successfully?

The feedback generated from these questions creates important "feed forward" information that you can act on to proactively address potential problems before they become major impediments.

24

ONBOARDING DAY SIXTY

TIME TO PIVOT? READJUSTING TO THE "REAL" JOB

The sixty-day window also represents unique challenges in onboarding new hires. By this time, they've made friends, familiarized themselves with the organization's key leaders and systems, and developed a rhythm that they've hopefully made their own. Interestingly enough, sixty days is also enough time to see if any of their peers have drawn lines in the sand, challenged them in any way, or developed cliques that exclude new hires from participation.

At this stage, performance tends to show itself, but just as important, conduct begins to come into play. For example, if the new hire is a strong team builder, people leader, or system challenger, those traits will have shown themselves by now. Likewise, if she's made friends and now has lunch buddies or tends to keep to herself despite others going out to lunch every day, those traits come into play in this important two-month window.

While there are no right or wrong answers to issues surrounding sociability, camaraderie, and willingness to make herself part of the group, it's important to determine if the new hire is made to feel welcome and comfortable in the new environment. Likewise, does she welcome others to approach her and feel comfortable dealing with her at this important interval? Issues regarding role expectations and personality matches often surface at the sixty-day review, so look for conduct- and behavior-related markers that may show themselves at this juncture. If you don't ask, you may never know.

Following are sample questions that may help you get this conversation off on the right foot when you sit down for your one-on-one follow-up meeting.

SIXTY-DAY ONE-ON-ONE FOLLOW-UP QUESTIONS

Do you have enough, too much, or too little time to do your work?

Do you have access to the appropriate tools and resources? Do you feel you have been sufficiently trained in all aspects of your job to perform at a high level?

How do you see your job relating to the organization's mission and vision?

What do you need to learn to improve? What can the organization do to help you become more successful in your role?

Compare the organization to what we explained it would be like when you initially interviewed with us. Have you experienced any surprises, disappointments, or other "aha" moments that you're comfortable sharing?

How does it go when your supervisor offers constructive criticism or corrects your work?

How have your relationships with your peers developed over the last sixty days? Have you been made to feel welcome, and do you think you've made others feel welcome in partnering with you?

Is there anything I can help with? Can I support you with anything at this point to help you continue to onboard and integrate into our organization more successfully?

25

ONBOARDING DAY NINETY

INITIAL GOAL SETTING AND ALIGNING EXPECTATIONS FOR QUARTERLY CHECK-INS FOR YEAR ONE AND BEYOND

The ninety-day pulse check-in meeting represents a conclusion as well as a new beginning: a conclusion to the onboarding process and a go-forward strategy that sets expectations for quarterly check-ins that the employee sets with you, her manager.

First, let's consider the look-back questions to ensure that the entire onboarding process went as smoothly as possible. Then, let's look at the feed-forward questions and issues you'll want to address to establish a quarterly rhythm for performance feedback, goal attainment, and celebration.

PART 1: LOOK-BACK QUESTIONS

The primary focus of your ninety-day meeting with your new hires should be on developing their understanding of the business, its key players, and its current initiatives. What are the higher-level goals that your company is focusing on, and how does each person's role contribute to those goals? What opportunities exist where new hires can make a difference? The following questions can help assess the past three months' experiences:

What questions do you have about our business, industry, or current initiatives that may still cause some confusion?

Who on the senior leadership team have you had an opportunity to connect with one-on-one over the last three months? Who would you still like to meet?

Which coworkers have been helpful since you arrived? (Goal: pinpoint which employees can be influential in retaining new hires.)

Who do you talk to when you have questions about your work? Do you feel comfortable asking?

Have you had any uncomfortable situations or conflicts with supervisors, coworkers, or customers?

How would you rate leadership communication overall on a scale from one to ten (with ten being highest)?

Do you believe your ideas and suggestions are valued? Give me some examples.

In retrospect, what could we have done differently in terms of setting your expectations appropriately for working in our company overall and for your job specifically?

PART 2: FEED-FORWARD QUESTIONS

Let's move forward with the understanding that we'll meet formally once per quarter to discuss your professional and career progress as well as attainment of your goals. I'd like you to schedule time on my calendar for those quarterly update meetings, and they're strictly for you to run as you see fit. I'll be here to coach and help, but I want you to take the lead. Does that sound reasonable? [*Yes.*]

I'd like us to develop specific goals at our month-six meeting. We can discuss them as we get closer to that date, but I'm open to suggestions any time along the way.

Overall, when we get together at these three-month intervals, I'd like to hear how you're progressing toward your annual goals, if any goals need to be adjusted, whether you require additional support in terms of resources or training, and how your career interests tie into your work. I'll also ask you to focus on your professional development needs when we have our quarterly one-on-ones and also let me know if we need to pivot or change direction altogether because of changes that come our way. Does that sound like a good plan? [*Yes.*]

Great. Consider these quarterly touch-base meetings a part of your annual performance review so there won't be any surprises along the way. Can you make that commitment to me going forward? [*Yes.*]

Okay then, I'll defer to you to schedule the next meeting at month six by sending me a calendar invite. I won't remind you, though—I don't feel that's necessary—but I want you to stick to this quarterly review program until it's time for your annual review. At that point, we'll establish our team's newest goals, and then we can work together to modify them to reflect your own particular performance goals. Here are the types of questions I'll likely ask you at the six-month mark:

What two or three performance goals make sense in light of your first half-year of experience at our company?

What would you change or amend in terms of your target goals or timelines to ensure you're remaining on track?

Is any additional training or education required to help you meet your goals?

Do you see any stretch opportunities or areas where you'd like to assume additional responsibilities or gain broader exposure?

[*Optional*] Are you interested in being considered for our "high-potential" program or gaining cross-training in any other parts of the business?

How will you plan to strengthen your capabilities in the areas of leadership, communication, and teambuilding?

What can I do to help you meet your goals or otherwise assist you with your own career and professional development?

The end result: better performance, clearer expectations, improved engagement, and ideally, stronger retention. After all, it stands to reason that employees who are engaged in these types of activities from the first day will feel a stronger connection to you and your organization over time. They'll feel acknowledged, included, and more excited about their prospects for long-term success and commitment, so they'll likely demonstrate greater loyalty and productivity. What's interesting is that it won't even take that much time.

While traditional NEO may still last one full day, follow-up meetings on days thirty, sixty, and ninety may be scheduled for thirty minutes each. All in all, your total hour commitment may be little more than several hours per year per team member, but because the meetings are spread wisely over the new hire's ninety-day introductory period, the constant follow-up and ongoing contact help cement a relationship that will stand the test of time.

Is there an "opportunity cost" (that is, a downside or disadvantage) to removing the individual from the field at these various intervals? Of course there is, especially in terms of your time as well as the individual's ability to complete her work. But think of all you'll be gaining. You'll have a chance to identify your top performers, provide special assignments to those looking for more, spot individuals who may be challenged and need to course correct, and flag others who may not have been cast in the right role during the hiring process. Your extra attention will help new hires incorporate new concepts and skills into their natural learning process when the timing is right for them, and your extra set of eyes will identify opportunities that your organization may not have otherwise been aware of.

An extended onboarding program is a rare opportunity to help your organization maximize its investment in new hires and increase the chances for success. Employ this strategy for the next six months and measure your new-hire retention results as a before and after. Don't be surprised to see a superior return on this particular investment in your new hires' futures because of the time you'll invest, the opportunities you'll identify, and the ongoing commitment that will benefit your organization over the long haul.

Best of all, you can do this with your team even if your company doesn't have a broader onboarding program. That's the beauty of creating your own leadership ecosystem. Simply keep your boss in the loop so everyone's on the same page, and don't be surprised to see others mirroring your success. After all, great ideas are simply that, and when they show that they work well in practice, then others will likely follow suit. That's role-model leadership at its highest level, and this program can place you in the role of outstanding leader, communicator, and team builder from the very start.

REMOTE ONBOARDING

3D EXPERIENCES IN A 2D WORLD

The goal of virtual employee onboarding is the same as in-person onboarding. It helps your new hire get familiar with your organization and its mission and values, makes them feel welcomed and included, facilitates connections with the team, and provides them with the tools and training they need to start making an immediate impact. Without being able to meet in person, it can be challenging to make your new employee feel like part of the team.

Remote onboarding carries with it specific challenges relative to in-person onboarding. As in all things virtual, the investment in communication, structure, and direction must be more purposeful and intentional when onboarding virtual employees. After all, these new hires will be expected to produce and contribute just like everyone else—only without the one-on-one interpersonal contact that typically helps new hires adjust to a new environment and feel comfortable with social relationships that naturally develop quickly in person.

As such, your remote onboarding strategy needs a bit of a twist from the traditional model to reach the same level of success. True, you'll follow the same patterns and structure as outlined above in the Day One, Thirty, Sixty, and Ninety scenarios. However, your focus on the Day One experience must be tighter, more thought out, and deliberate to ensure a smooth onboarding experience. Here's how to build a personalized and engaging virtual onboarding experience that will prepare new hires for success.

STEP 1:
When possible, hire in cohorts rather than individually.

When new hires start together on the same day, they develop a natural bond and rely on one another, comparing notes and experiences and sharing initial insights. Leverage this important social element of new hire onboarding whenever the opportunity arises.

STEP 2:
Email new hires a welcome kit.

Include relevant information they need to know before their first day, such as when to expect equipment, the agenda for their first day and week, and links to join initial video conferences. You may also want to provide early access to your employee intranet for your new employee to explore prior to day one. Provide an organization chart and discuss the key leaders and their departments, especially those that interact closely with yours. Attach vocabulary lists that might shorten the learning curve, especially those that include industry jargon and acronyms that new hires will likely take months to learn on their own. Most important, make your new employee feel valued, appreciated, and part of the team by mailing them company swag (e.g., sweatshirt, coffee mug, pen and pad with company logo, and the like). You can also offer unique welcome gifts like a voucher for coffee or lunch delivery on their first day.

STEP 3:
Deliver work equipment on Day One.

Send new hires the tech equipment they need to be successful (e.g., laptop, mouse, keyboard, monitor, headset, and cell phone). If possible, download and install company-specific software and programs before sending any equipment to your new hire's home address. Include initial IT setup instructions to help new hires log onto their computer and work email for the first time. Likewise, because asynchronous and real-time online communication are both essential for a remote work environment, make sure your new hire is added to all the right calendar invites, pre-scheduled meetings, and email groups and messaging apps so they don't miss any important messages or updates. Give your new hires a "tour" of your virtual workspace. Schedule a virtual orientation with a member of your IT team to get your new hire set up with their technology and software (e.g., login credentials, VPN, and project management applications). Make this the first meeting of the new hire's day—especially since their only connection with your team will be through technology.

STEP 4:
Inform your current team of the new hire's arrival.

Send a new employee announcement to inform your team of the new hire's arrival. Make sure to copy the new employees so they can see any welcome messages or GIFs their new teammates send. You can also announce their arrival in a #general channel on Slack or during team meetings to give them a warm welcome. Set up virtual job shadowing or job training sessions to help new employees learn their new role, or to get a higher-level understanding of what other teams and departments do.

STEP 5:
Assign a coach or mentor
(aka "welcome buddy") from Day One.

Creating a connection right away to a peer or senior member of the team is a great investment of everyone's time—both the new hire's and the mentor's. As discussed throughout Part 4, it provides an excellent opportunity for you to develop your team members' leadership potential, it aligns your bench strength in terms of identifying high potential leaders, and it creates a sheltered transition for the new hire to access a peer's time and expertise rather than only the manager's. A welcome buddy can also introduce your new hire to the right people and share information, tips, and advice to help them settle in and be productive sooner.

STEP 6:
Create an agenda for the first week.

What would you like your new hire to learn and do during their first week? Come up with a schedule for their first week, making sure to build in breaks between video calls and enough check-ins and touchpoints so they don't feel ignored or overlooked. A simple checklist can help tremendously, allowing new hires to "attack" the required elements at their own pace and discretion.

STEP 7:
Build flexibility into the first week's meetings and gatherings.

Avoid "Zoom fatigue" by tailoring digital onboarding material for the most impact. Adjust your language for a digital format, add more detail, and create content in different formats (e.g., PDFs, 1:1

training/screensharing, online training videos, IMs, and good old-fashioned phone calls).

STEP 8:
Schedule group or one-on-one meetings with other team members starting on Day Two and throughout the first week.

Discuss backgrounds and personal interests, "one interesting thing to know about me" kinds of activities, favored methods of communication, and the general way of doing things. Have current employees go around and briefly explain what they do, including a fun fact about themselves.

Conversations like this often evolve into discussions concerning current projects and upcoming celebrations, which is a healthy way to launch new relationships. Having one-on-one time with an immediate supervisor, mentor, and peers envelops the new hire immediately in an environment of care and engagement. Help your new employee get to know the team in a more casual setting by scheduling virtual team lunches for the first week. (No handshakes or picking up the tab required.)

STEP 9:
Assign required training by the beginning of Week Two.

But be careful not to inundate new hires with excessive training requirements. On the other hand, there's no reason to wait when it comes to checking off training obligations. Whether new hires are required to attend respect-in-the-workplace training, code-of-conduct instruction, or engage in remote ergonomic assessments of their workstations, implement these training programs right away so that everything can be completed by the end of Month One. Allow new hires to work through certain onboarding materials at their own pace by offering text resources and videos they can browse through independently.

STEP 10:
Create space for questions.

I generally recommend one-on-one meetings with all direct reports every week, but in cases of remote onboarding, meetings should be scheduled daily at preset times. Of course, a new hire can pick up the phone or instant-message you at any time, but remote setups require lots of communication and contact in the first week. The added touch-base meetings will come in very handy in that first week.

STEP 11:
Build in spontaneity.

Spontaneous interactions between coworkers can help new hires build connections with their team and gain a better understanding of the company culture. In an office setting, random conversations usually happen when grabbing coffee, waiting for a conference room to clear, or when passing by a coworker's desk. In a remote environment, these spur-of-the-moment interactions have to be more intentional. Find opportunities to spark conversations between your new hire and the rest of the team. If your company uses Slack, for example, you can use the Donut integration to pair your new hire with people across the company for virtual coffee meetups. Whatever the case and whatever the technology, ensure that enough connectivity is built in to create multiple opportunities for personal engagement and getting to know one another.

STEP 12:
Collect virtual onboarding feedback.

Make your new hires feel valued and heard beyond their first day and initial few weeks. Send a survey to collect feedback about your virtual onboarding process.

Onboarding is among the most influential factors when it comes to employee experience. But creating a great onboarding experience isn't easy. Like many other processes in remote teams, onboarding requires a lot more deliberate consideration compared to how in-person co-located teams operate. Create a list of each step in the onboarding process and ensure that the new hire doesn't get lost under the avalanche of new information, especially if they work in another time zone. Simply stated, look for every opportunity to build trust and inclusion from the very first day. Your investment in remote onboarding will provide long-term returns on your initial investment.

The questions that follow can stand alone or be used in tandem with the regular questions you ask candidates in these various stages of pre- and postemployment. What's important is that you have a set of questions handy to address the unique needs of a remote team. Incorporate some of the questions that follow into your onboarding questionnaires at days thirty, sixty, and ninety to ensure that you are addressing the key needs of this critical population:

What suggestions do you have to make the team feel more collegial? Since we don't have a proverbial watercooler to stand around, what can we do to get to know one another better on a more personal level? Would a weekly remote team lunch where we only talk about non-work matters make sense for us?

What can we do to create trust behind the computer and develop a greater sense of having one another's backs?

Are we generally available enough and accessible to one another?

Are there any features in our current lineup of communications tools that we're not using that would help us respond more quickly and generally be more available to one another?

How does work-life integration work for you in your remote working relationship? Are you able to cut ties with your work at day's end or do you find it difficult to separate yourself from your work when there are no clear boundaries (like leaving the office at the end of the day)?

Would you add or subtract to the number of standing meetings we typically all attend in a given week? Do you have any suggestions on how to tighten our communication chain without adding more meetings?

Do you at times feel isolated, disengaged, or disconnected from the rest of the team? If not, have you noticed any of your peers who might be feeling that way so we can support them better?

How can we better maintain a sense of connection when we're all remote? Do you feel our culture is being enriched because of our intentional focus on making it work remotely, or is the remoteness detracting from our culture overall?

How can we strengthen a culture of trust, adopt an achievement mindset, and better manage change? If you could add one thing to our team's culture that would help along the lines of incorporating and mastering change, what would it be?

[*Optional*] No brownie points here, but how would you grade me on a scale of one to ten (with ten being highest) in the areas of leadership, communication, and teambuilding?

[*Optional*] Do you prefer working on-site in the office or working remotely from home? If you could choose one option exclusively, which would it be and why?

Do you believe you're able to do your best work every day? Does the remote setup help along those lines or hinder your ability to do so?

What can we do to have more fun? Would a monthly business book club help? Would it make sense to add a weekly recap meeting on Fridays at 3:00 p.m. to relax and unwind as we roll up to the weekend?

The key difference between working on-site and working remotely is that, as a leader, you have to be more intentional in terms of what you're trying to achieve through your people. What happens naturally when human beings congregate—friendship, camaraderie, and trust—can be harder and take much longer to develop when your team is working remotely, sometimes spread over different time zones and parts of the world.

Look to mastering remote leadership by simply practicing selfless leadership: put others' needs ahead of your own, ask for people's input because you genuinely care about their well-being, and be sure they know that you're there for them. Lead with your heart, demonstrate empathy and genuine concern for the special needs of this particular population, and solicit their feedback at every turn.

You'll likely find that others will emulate your role-model leadership and develop strong remote leadership qualities and capabilities of their own.

■　■　■

Effective interviewing and hiring are likely the most important tools in your leadership tool kit. Done right, you'll hone your skills at identifying top talent, making high-probability hires, and onboarding them successfully. What typically stands in the way of corporate leaders mastering the hiring process is a lack of questions to ask at varying points along the way—whether during initial telephone screens and in-person interviews, during the reference-checking phone calls with candidates' prior supervisors, during offer negotiations, or while onboarding. You're now equipped with the tools and techniques to master this timely and complex process.

Build your skills, play with interview questions to see which ones work for you, remain in contact once candidates give notice at their current employers, and see the extended onboarding process as an opportunity to set goals and discuss career and professional development with your teams. When done correctly, it's a seamless process that extends from effective hiring to performance management and then to leadership development. What's amazing is that this doesn't take much *additional* time—it simply makes better use of your existing time. Thank you for allowing me to join you in this exciting path toward stronger hiring—you'll likely find that few other leadership activities or endeavors will reap a better return on investment for your time and energy.

INDEX

ABOUT THE AUTHOR

Paul Falcone (www.PaulFalconeHR.com) is the chief human resources officer (CHRO) of the Motion Picture and Television Fund in Woodland Hills, California, where he's responsible for all aspects of HR leadership and strategy. He's the former CHRO of the Nickelodeon Animation Studios and head of international human resources for Paramount Pictures in Hollywood. Paul served as head of HR for the TV production unit of NBCUniversal, where he oversaw HR operations for NBC's late night and primetime programming lineup, including *The Tonight Show*, *Saturday Night Live*, and *The Office*. Paul is a renowned expert on effective interviewing and hiring, performance management, and leadership development, especially in terms of helping companies build higher-performing leadership teams. He also has extensive experience in healthcare/biotech and financial services across international, nonprofit, and union environments.

Paul is the author of a number of HarperCollins Leadership, AMACOM, and SHRM books, many of which have been ranked on Amazon as #1 bestsellers in the areas of human resources management, labor and employment law, business mentoring and coaching, communication in management, and business decision-making and problem-solving. Bestselling books like *101 Tough Conversations to Have with Employees*, *101 Sample Write-Ups for Documenting Employee Performance Problems*, and *96 Great Interview Questions to Ask Before You Hire* have been translated into Chinese, Vietnamese, Korean, Indonesian, and Turkish.

Paul is a certified executive coach through the Marshall Goldsmith Stakeholder Centered Coaching program, a long-term contributor to SHRM.org and *HR Magazine*, and an adjunct faculty member in UCLA Extension's School of Business and Management, where he's taught courses on workplace ethics, recruitment and selection, legal aspects of human resources management, and international human resources. He is an accomplished keynote presenter, inhouse trainer, and webinar facilitator in the areas of talent management and effective leadership communication.